MARKET

MARKETING TO WIN

How Small Businesses Can Do More With Less

JACQUELINE BIGGS

R3THINK PRESS

First Published in Great Britain 2013 by Rethink Press

Illustrations by Vladislava

Testimonials

'Marketing to Win' is a must-read for business owners who want to understand the fundamentals of marketing and thrive in today's competitive environment. Full of useful advice and practical examples, you'll end up with powerful ideas that will boost your business.
Valerie Khoo, award-winning serial entrepreneur and author of
Power Stories: The 8 Stories You MUST Tell to Build an Epic Business,
www.ValerieKhoo.com

Jacqueline is the person I go to when I want expert advice on how to market anything online. A must read for all small business owners.
Shaa Wasmund, Founder, www.smarta.com,
author of *Stop Talking Start Doing*

This book is an accessible treasure trove for SME's looking to develop their brand. It is packed with a wealth of ideas for improving your marketing effectiveness, and many of the tips can be immediately implemented. Highly recommended.
Shireen Smith, LLB LLM, Founder of Azrights Solicitors, and expert in Intellectual Property Law and Online Branding,
www.ip-brands.com

Excellent, read today and do it right tomorrow! What every entrepreneur and business leader needs to know about marketing and how to get it done.
Sam Dyson, CEO, www.LuxuryLocations.com

The perfect read for entrepreneurial business owners who crave a competitive advantage. I only wish this book had been written 8 years ago when I was starting up. The shocking statistics around the failure of new enterprises make this book a must read. Jacqueline's story is refreshing. There are techniques in this book that every business owner could and should put into practice; I did, and I'm already seeing results.
Rob Bloxham, MD, www.thisisorb.com

This is the must-have book for the business owner, line manager and modern marketer. It informs and educates you on the key trends and changes needed to succeed in today's decentralised business environment. This book has focused our marketing needs and given us a simple to follow set of action points and plans. This is the most comprehensive review of marketing techniques available and you won't put it down once you start reading.

Nigel Quantick, CEO, www.GroupSetUp.com

A stunning birds-eye view into the world of marketing for business from a creative expert tuned into the right frequency of this current global market.

Devron Cariba, MD, www.WriteMyBid.com

This book is a great read for any small to medium sized company, that wants to get to grips with marketing its products and services in a way that will truly accelerate growth. It unveils the shroud of secrecy around marketing and strategies for developing successful businesses.

Mary Murray, Executive Coach, www.MaryMurrayCoaching.com

When I first met Jacqueline, I knew she had the knowledge and the drive to make a lasting difference in the entrepreneurial world. Now that I've read this book, I know exactly how her inspiring vision to reduce the ratio of small businesses failing in the UK will come to fruition. I meet several dozen tech start-up owners every week and see how excellent products don't get commercialised because of a lack of marketing expertise. Jacqueline lays out the basics of what it takes to succeed in any market, in a way that makes it easy to understand and fun to implement in your business. This book will make a huge difference to the small and start-up business scene UK wide.

Paulina Sygulska, Director, GrantTree, www.GrantTree.co.uk

Contents

About the author

 Jacqueline Biggs has been a marketing strategist for fourteen years. For ten of these Jacqueline worked with a number of FTSE 100 brands including Intel, Scottish and Newcastle, Glaxo-SmithKline, Reckitt Benckiser, Procter & Gamble and Kellogg's whist at Euro RSCG and M&C Saatchi advertising agencies in Sydney, New York and London. In 2009, Jacqueline launched Blue Lemons, a results focused marketing agency for start-ups and small to medium sized businesses. Jacqueline realised that all the tips and strategies she had learned and created for corporate brands could be applied to start-ups and small companies and generate extraordinary results on very small budgets. Blue Lemons is renowned for helping business owners to deliver the right message, to the right audience in the most effective way, whether on or offline.

In 2011, Jacqueline co-founded Brand Camp for entrepreneurs with Rob Bloxham, together they run events and online courses on all aspects of marketing and brand development ranging from how to create and build a successful brand, to how to make money from social media.

Jacqueline is known for delivering real results and making her clients feel wildly optimistic about their business' future.

CONNECT WITH JACQUELINE

t @jacquelinebiggs

f facebook.com/BrandCampCommunity

in uk.linkedin.com/in/jacquelinebiggs

e jacqueline@jacquelinebiggs.com

W www.jacquelinebiggs.com (book resources)
www.blue-lemons.com (marketing agency)
www.brand-camp.com (marketing courses)

GETTING STARTED

Introduction

> "The only way to do great work is to love
> what you do. If you haven't found it yet,
> keep looking and don't settle, as with any
> matter of the heart, you will know when
> you find it and it just gets better and better
> as the years roll on."
> **Steve Jobs**

THE ONLY WAY TO DO GREAT WORK IS TO LOVE WHAT YOU DO. THE OTHER WAY...

I came to and realised I was lying face down in the road and someone was standing over me, telling me not to move as they put a neck brace on me. I heard other voices, but couldn't really make out what was happening. Without realising it, I was drifting in and out of consciousness. Next thing I knew, I was in an ambulance, lying on a stretcher whizzing through London with the siren blaring. I was told I had been hit by a car, as I crossed the road to enter Tottenham Court Road station. It was about 10pm on Wednesday April 7th, 2004.

At the time, I worked crazy hours in an advertising agency as a strategy planner and it was yet another late night at the office. Work was often a relentless cycle of late nights and no weekends. That was the price I paid for a job I loved. Ambitious and hungry for success, my career was my life.

I had fractured my jaw in two places, shattered my elbow, cut my head open and torn my anterior cruciate ligament. I needed immediate and multiple surgeries, quickly. Unfortunately, one of the operations went tragically wrong and I ended up on a life support machine due to a complication. My parents had just arrived at the hospital and faced the reality that I might not make it; the police had contacted them a few hours after my accident and an incredibly kind neighbour had driven them to the hospital in the early hours. They had braced themselves for the worst, but still didn't expect this. All they could do was hope and pray I'd make it.

After a stressful twenty-four hours I eventually pulled through and as the haze of the morphine began to wear off days later, I began to reflect on the immense perspective on life a near fatal accident gives you. If (and I hope you never do) you have a moment when your life flashes before you, it really does change everything. I had no idea if I was going to fully recover. I had plates in my face, pins in my arm and a bolt in my knee. As I was unable to even get up to go the bathroom, it was days before I saw my own reflection. When I eventually did, I was in a state of shock, I did not recognise my own face. I was horrified by what was reflected back at me and burst into floods of tears. Even now, as I write this, that terrifying moment is still so vivid it brings tears to my eyes, over eight years later. Nothing prepares you for it. My amazing parents and family had never once let on that I looked anything other than normal when they visited me day in and day out. Only years later did my parents confess that when they arrived at the Accident and Emergency department of the hospital and were taken to me, they didn't recognise me, as my facial injuries were so severe. Desperate for reassurance, I asked to see the maxillo-facial consultant (the guy who special-ises in facial injuries) and he assured me that when the swelling and bruising went down, the pins would pull my face back into shape. That was easy for him to say.

He was, thankfully, right, but it was several months before I resembled the old me. As the bruising came out, my face went from purple, to blue, to green to yellow, but it was only when the swelling subsided that I could start to see myself in my face again.

I had a lot of time to reflect on what I wanted out of life while I recovered in hospital. I loved working in Advertising, but I realised that I didn't feel rewarded enough by what I did. The big multinational clients I had worked on like Intel, Reckitt Benckiser, Jean Paul Gaultier and Paul Smith were already hugely successful and my role was to help them to grow even bigger. It suddenly didn't seem worthwhile. As I thought through my options, I realised that I wanted to do something that really made a difference. There were lots of start-ups and small businesses that were really struggling and given my experience, I could really help them to grow their businesses. I decided that I would help companies that really needed 'big agency' guidance, but could not afford it. They would however, be able to afford me. The more I thought about it, the more excited I got about my new focus. Helping to shape a company in the early years is incredibly exciting. However, as I only had five years' experience helping to build businesses, I decided to hone my skills for a couple more, learning from a true master.

I applied for a strategic planning role at M&C Saatchi's advertising agency in London working on what were then Scottish and Newcastle brands; Foster's and Kronenbourg 1664 (now Heineken owned) and GlaxoSmithKline's Lucozade Sport brands. The chance to learn from someone like Maurice Saatchi was an exciting prospect. In addition, the brands were launching new product lines, so I could then use everything I learned about how to create, launch and build successful brands to help entrepreneurs turn their ideas into successful businesses. The more I researched the entrepreneurial world, the more it excited me. I was shocked by the statistics that showed that every year 270,000[1] businesses started in the UK and four out of five[2] of these failed! How could this be? Further research revealed two critical reasons – they didn't

1   http://techcrunch.com/2011/03/28/uk-entrepreneurs-launch-startupbritain-with-government-backing-but-not-money/
2   http://news.bbc.co.uk/1/hi/business/7759207.stm

understand the financials of their business and they didn't have a clear business plan. I knew I could help.

I've been running a consultancy, working with passionate entrepreneurs and small business owners since 2009. So that I can help a broader number of businesses, in 2011 I launched Brand Camp with Rob Bloxham, a phenomenal branding expert. We offer group training and on-going educational programmes in all aspects of business and marketing. We have hand-picked a team of experts to work alongside us and together we ensure small businesses in the UK have the right knowledge and tools to be successful. We are on a mission to reverse the trend of failure for so many businesses in the UK. It's exciting, daunting and very rewarding.

I now wholeheartedly agree with Steve Jobs' quote at the start of this chapter. Had my accident not happened, I would still be working in an advertising agency helping the fat cats get fatter. There's nothing wrong with that of course, it's just not for me. Instead, I've created an inspiring mission that others want to get behind and support.

So that I can help more entrepreneurs, more quickly, I decided to write this book. My objective is to save you time, money and effort. Consider this book a short-cut to help you avoid the costly mistakes that are an unfortunate rite of passage for most entrepreneurs with little or no marketing experience. This book will help you to do what you do brilliantly and show you how to do it faster and smarter. In short, I will help you to do more with less.

I will teach you some of the strategies employed by multi-million-pound companies and I will show you how to apply them to your small business. If you follow some of the strategies that I outline in this book, you will recoup the price of this book hundreds of times over. But I don't just want you to follow *some* of them; why not focus on applying *all* of them to your business? You might just put a rocket under it...

How to get the most out of this book

> "In any situation, the best thing you can do is the right thing; the next best thing you can do is the wrong thing; the worst thing you can do is nothing."
>
> **Theodore Roosevelt**

This book does require you to take action. If you are not prepared to do that, please put this book back on the shelf until you are.

I mean that!

At the end of some of the chapters you will find a series of actions. Try and complete these before reading on, as it is always harder to go back. Sure you can read the book from cover to cover and claim you'll go back and complete them later, but we both know it doesn't work like that. If you want to get the most out of this book, then complete the exercises as you go through, rather than put them off.

This book has an accompanying website which contains extended information on some of the topics I cover. There are helpful videos, articles and tips to further your learning. Connect with me, share what's working, what's not, what you're struggling with and I'll help you with any challenges.

Before you get started, I want to let you in on a secret. For years, people have been over complicating business with theories and new ideas that claim to 'revolutionise' the way we run companies, but within a year or two they just disappear. In reality, business is simple. You just need to get the basics right. I want to help you do just that.

The worst thing you could do, when you finish this book is to do nothing and tell no-one else about it. Please complete the actions, then pass it on, buy it as a gift or share your highlighted kindle notes on your blog. 240,000 businesses launch each year in the UK and four out of five fail; this needs to stop. Play your part and help other businesses to get the basics right and not become a statistic.

To check out the accompanying website, please go to www.jacquelinebiggs.com

PATHWAY TO PROFIT

Need this
10% strategy

Why it's easier than you think to grow your business

> "Whether you think you can or think you can't, you're right."
>
> **Henry Ford**

I truly believe that marketing is easy. No, it's not just because I've been doing it successfully for fourteen years. It's because once you understand a few principles, it really is easy. Without realising it, you are sitting on myriad of opportunities and I just want to open your eyes and show you how you can turn these into profits. Marketing is part big ideas and part process, you're an entrepreneur, you have the ideas, so I am going to help you with the process part. I hope that this next example will help you realise that it's a lot easier than you think to step-change your business.

THE 10% STRATEGY ✳

I want to show you how a small increase in key metrics in your business has the potential to create a huge impact in net profits.

Katrina is the owner of a spray-tanning salon and in her first year she generated 1,000 new business leads through her marketing and converted 10% of these, 100, into paying customers. On average, each customer spent £100 on a spray tan multi-buy deal and bought this deal ten times, over the course of the year. Note this spray tan business is based in Essex, where the Oompa Loompa look is all the rage. So Katrina's business turned over £100,000 over the course of the year and, with a profit margin of 30%, Katrina's net profit was £30,000.

This year, Katrina is following the '10% strategy', she is going to increase the volume of leads she generates by 10%, increase her conversion rate by 10%, increase her average order value by 10% and increase her profit margin by 10% by decreasing her costs. The '10% strategy' sounds and is entirely manageable and when you look at the cumulative effect of this strategy on her net profit, you will really begin to get excited. So, a 10% increase on the volume of leads means she will generate 1,100 new business leads this year, a 10% increase on her conversion rate means she needs to convert 11% of these into paying customers, which results in 121 customers. She then needs to increase the average spend by 10%, so each customer needs to spend around £110. A 10% increase on the number of purchases customers make each year, means they need to buy 11 times rather than 10. This means that she will then turnover £146,410 this year, almost 50% increase on last year:

121 customers x £110 (average spend) x
11 (no of purchases / yr) = £146,410

If she successfully increases her profit margin by 10%, raising it to 33%, her net profit will be £48,315, which is a 61% increase on last year. Wow! This is a very powerful and effective strategy for any business. You might think this all sounds very easy in theory but in reality it's hard to make these incremental changes. However, what you will discover in the following chapters of this book is how you can make this strategy work in your business with step-by-step examples. The role of this book is to help you to identify ways to improve your marketing so that you can experience this positive trickle-down effect in your business. At the end of this book, I revisit this model and categorise each of the strategies that I cover according to how they can increase each key metric; leads, conversions, average order value and average volume of yearly purchases.

Failure is not a dirty word

> "I've missed more than 9,000 shots in my career. I've lost almost 300 games. Twenty-six times, I've been trusted to take the game-winning shot and missed. I've failed over and over and over again in my life. And that is why I succeed."
>
> **Michael Jordan**

As a nation, we take failing pretty badly. At school we're repeatedly told how important it is to get it right; we're marked-down for getting it wrong. Those who soar through the education system do so because they're right more than they're wrong. Those who don't succeed at school are viewed negatively as failures and dropouts. For many, there's an accepted path we're expected to take:

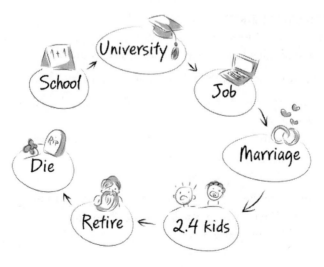

The expected path is to be a cog in a wheel, it's well trodden, safe and responsible, though if you ask me that's simply a euphemism for 'more people to blame' for any lack of success. It was great to watch people's reaction when I decided to exchange life as a cog for that of a business owner. It was usually met with a sharp intake of breath, as it made people feel uncomfortable, why on earth would I not take the safe path? Tales of failures, bankruptcy and general woe quickly followed. It's interesting how few Brits celebrate and encourage mavericks and change-makers. Luckily I was pretty focused on making my dent on the universe.

The fact that you're reading this book means there's also a high chance that you don't agree with the above chain of events either. You've already discovered that there is another way. You know that for many a job really means Just-Over-Broke and you want to create change in the world by taking a different path. Great!

However, I'm guessing you're still not comfortable with failure. Very few British entrepreneurs are, it is something in our genetic make up that we need to override. I'd like to try and make you a little more comfortable with the fact that it's not just OK to fail, to be truly successful you need to fail. In fact, you need to fail faster to succeed more.

FAMOUS FAILURES

Before you read on, spend a minute naming five famous millionaire or billionaire entrepreneurs of any nationality.

Chances are, some of the following featured in your list:

- ❑ Donald Trump - bankrupt in 1990, now worth well over $3billion
- ❑ Richard Branson - Remember Virgin Vodka or Virgin Jeans?
- ❑ Michael Dell didn't get a degree
- ❑ Steve Jobs dropped-out of college
- ❑ Bill Gates is one of Harvard's most successful drop-outs
- ❑ Mark Zuckerburg is also a Harvard drop-out and is the world's youngest billionaire[3]

3   Time.com: Top 10 college dropouts

All of these were 'failures' - they didn't finish school, they went bankrupt, their ideas backfired. However, today, they are heralded as role models; successful entrepreneurs that have made more money than it's possible to spend. When you talk to each of them, they are so grateful for their failure, as it's the very reason they are where they are today.

BIG BUSINESSES GET IT WRONG TOO

Many big multi-nationals are comfortable with failure, in fact it's considered a stepping stone, as failing fast is usually the secret to innovation success. You might argue that they have a financial buffer, as they are successful in other areas, but they too had to start somewhere and it's the attitude that counts.

There's a famous anecdote about the attitude to failure of Tom Watson Jr, the head of IBM. Watson had called a Vice President (VP) to his office to discuss a failed development project that lost IBM about $10 million. Expecting to be fired, the VP took his letter of resignation with him. Watson just shook his head: "You are certainly not leaving after we just gave you a $10 million education." Failure was not seen as a problem at IBM, as long as it was turned into a learning experience.

Richard Branson also embraces failure. According to his publisher, John Brown, "The secret of (Branson's) success is his failures. He keeps opening things and a good many of them fail but he doesn't care. He keeps on going."

What's more, a failure in one way, can often open up new possibilities:

Champagne was invented by a monk called Dom Perignon when a bottle of wine accidentally had a secondary fermentation.

3M invented glue that was a failure, as it didn't stick. But it became the basis for the Post-it note, which is a huge success.

Pfizer tested Viagra, a new drug to relieve blood pressure. Whilst it was a failure at stopping high blood pressure, it had one beneficial side effect for the men in the group; it had a dramatic effect on their sexual vigour. Viagra is without doubt one of the most successful failures of all time.

Failure can be the mother of all innovation and as an entrepreneur you need to embrace this. However, ideally you want to create 'intelligent failures', those that fail early, inexpensively and create new insights into your target audience. Not always easy of course.

How to tell a brilliant idea from a dud!

> "The key to evangelism is a great product.
> It is easy, almost unavoidable to catalyse
> evangelism for a great product. It is hard to
> catalyse evangelism for crap."
> **Guy Kawasaki**

So when is a good idea, a good idea and not a complete waste of time? How can you ever know if you've struck gold or had the worst idea in the world? Whether you are adding a new product or service to your portfolio or launching a new company, the answer is simple. You have to research it. Woe betide the entrepreneur that locks himself away creating something "wonderful" and launches it in all its fully formed glory to the market. The chance of failure is so high. Research is an entrepreneur's best friend and it doesn't have to be expensive. Sadly, it's not fail proof, but it's a very good place to start.

KEY REASONS INNOVATIONS FAIL

There tend to be four big reasons that innovations fail in the market place, but there are some steps you can take to try to avoid falling foul of them.

1. They don't solve a genuine consumer problem

It's vital to research what your consumers want before you start innovating. Never assume you know. Exploratory research is key to identifying unmet or unarticulated desires. Whatever you're creating has to solve an important and relevant problem for your target audience.

Solution: Run a few focus groups with your target consumers and ask them how existing products and services could be improved; show them a prototype if you have one, or talk them through your concept to get feedback. Depending on what you need to research, it's also useful to create an online survey using tools like Survey Monkey or Survey Gizmo. However, don't let a survey be your only means of research, it's very important to have actual conversations with your intended audience, as this can often reveal critical insights a survey can miss.

A word of caution: It's very difficult to research completely new concepts with consumers - as Henry Ford famously said:

"If I asked people what they wanted, they would have said a faster horse"

It's important to use research as guide, but to go with your gut. Just make sure that whatever you create or produce solves a genuine problem, otherwise no one will want to buy what you have to sell.

2. They take too long to get to market and, or, the need has changed

Few organisations have a well-oiled innovation process, so it can take years to get a product to market and despite identifying previously unmet desires, the market changes and the window of opportunity is missed.

Solution: This is tough, but you need to do what you can to speed-up the process as much as possible and keep a constant eye on the market. Identify non competing companies that have gone through a similar process and chat to them about their key learnings. Alternatively, find a mentor to help you speed up your time to market by leveraging their contacts and experience.

3. They are poorly launched

Just because you've identified an unmet desire and created a product or service to meet it, does not mean that people will come flooding. You have to get the word out and give the launch adequate support. Apple is the master at product launches - Steve Jobs always presented a hugely anticipated product, as excitement had been building for weeks.

Solution: Study Apple's launch strategy, what can you learn from it and apply to your own? Clearly you're not Apple, so there will be much less hype and significantly less budget, but there is a lot you can learn from their approach, particularly from the way they build excitement and anticipation around the launch. If you have a small budget you will need to find creative ways to make a big impact with your launch. Watch out for stories in the media that you could piggy-back to get PR, or upcoming events targeting your audience that you could leverage.

4. They require too much work to adopt

Creating a change in behaviour is not easy. If the effort to change from an existing brand is considered high, it is not straightforward to encourage customers to switch, even when you have a better product at a lower price. You have to make it easy and if it's not, then you will struggle unless you are able to offer significant benefits. This is one of the biggest challenges you will face.

Solution: Review the market positioning of each of the products or services you are trying to replace. Explore all possible barriers to adoption and find ways to overcome them. Focus on making adoption as easy as possible.

Remember that failure is not a dirty word, it's feedback. If things don't go according to plan first time, then analyse why, learn from it and move on to create something bigger and better. Success is about going from failure to failure without losing your enthusiasm.

Intelligent Parenting® ✓
.co.uk ✓
.com ✓

It's called what???

> "Lady Gaga is my name. If you know me,
> and you call me Stefani, you don't
> really know me at all."
> **Lady Gaga**

Finding the right name for your brand, product or service is notoriously difficult. It's not enough to come up with a great name, you need to make sure you can get the corresponding domain name and a .com at that! You also need to make sure that you can trademark it, which often gets forgotten. The .com domain name is important if you are serious about building a successful website over the long term. While directing traffic to a .net or .org is fine, owning and redirecting the .com is critical. Even if you don't want to build a website for it, it's an important defence strategy, as someone else will buy it. If your brand takes off and someone already has the .com domain, you will be competing with them for traffic and brand recognition. That said, practically every URL you can think of has been bought up by a squatter hoping that one day someone will pay them handsomely for their smart purchase. Hideously annoying, but you can't knock their entrepreneurial get up and go. If that is the case, then approach the owner of the .com before your brand takes off.

TYPES OF NAMES

When deciding on a name, there are various types to choose between:

- ❏ **A real name** - This could be yours, another founder's or even a fictitious character with a real sounding name, such as Aunt Bessie and her line of frozen foods.

- ❏ **A made-up name** - This is a great chance to be playful, as there are less boundaries, but it can take a LOT of marketing spend to get remembered. That said, it's a great opportunity to enter the national lexicon – the ultimate acceptance is when your brand name is used as a verb, like Google, Skype and Wii, but this doesn't happen overnight of course.

- ❏ **A conjoined name** - similar to the above, as you're creating a new word, but it combines two words to bring a new meaning, such as Microsoft, so called because of its core focus on micro computer software, and FedEx, an abbreviation of Federal Express.

- ❏ **A descriptive name** - Whilst great at describing effectively what you do, such as Pizza Hut and Lean Cuisine, these are notoriously difficult to get trademarked.

- ❏ **Abbreviations** - This could be the initials of founding partners, AMV – Abbot Mead Vickers, a global advertising agency, or simply the short version of the full brand name, for example UPS (United Parcel Service); or like IKEA, a combination, in this case constructed from an amalgam of his name (Ingvar Kamprad), the farm where he grew up (Elmtaryd), and his home town (Agunnaryd in Småland, South Sweden).

- ❏ **A metaphorical name** - These are words that convey meanings through association, for example Jaguars, which are known for their grace and pace and Apple, felt to be fun, spirited and not intimidating.

- ❏ **Onomatopoeia** - A name that sounds like whatever it refers to, such as KaBoom energy drink and Meow Mix.

Whichever you go for, it has to be memorable. Alliteration can help (think of Krispy Kreme, Bed, Bath & Beyond) as can rhyming (Crunch n Munch, Yellow Mellow). Your decision is ultimately led by the type of brand and association you want to create.

As a final check, make sure your name also meets the following criteria:

- ☑ Easy to spell and pronounce
- ☑ Short and snappy
- ☑ Likeable
- ☑ Distinctive
- ☑ Protectable - you need to be able to trademark it

ACTION

- ☑ Review the names for each of your existing products and services against the above criteria - how do they fare?

- ☑ If you have not trademarked your name and now realise that you can't, contact an intellectual property lawyer for advice.

One-Shop-Shop complete ✓ Solution to the potty training process.

The biggest mistake most entrepreneurs make and how to avoid it

> "I like to listen. I have learned a great deal from listening carefully. Most people never listen."
> **Ernest Hemingway**

There is one, simple principle that you have to follow in business. No matter your industry, product or service, it still applies, with no exceptions.

It really is very simple and once you know it, you won't forget it. Following this one principle will save you hundreds of thousands of pounds, plus a lot of unnecessary stress.

It will also guarantee your success.

So what is it?

"Find out what your market wants and give it to them."

Yes, it really is that simple.

So why do so many entrepreneurs try to sell people what they think they need and not what they want? I see it time and time again. This simple principle gets overlooked and forgotten.

It's really important to understand the distinction between what consumers need and what they want. A lot of people talk about the importance of "meeting consumers' needs" and it is, very frustratingly, often heralded as the key to running a successful company by people who should know better. Someone might know that they need to lose weight, but what they want is another cake. Many people know they need to reduce their carbon footprint, but they still want an overseas holiday. Providing what people need is no guarantee that you will find demand. You have to give them what they want, not what you believe they need. If you want to help someone reduce their carbon footprint, don't lecture them and suggest they stay at home, help them to off-set their footprint through other means.

The same is true in the business to business market. I've had many frustrated clients who cannot understand why their clients don't buy their products or services when they are significantly better than the other alternatives on the market. They can prove it and they have endless case studies and testimonials to back it up. What's more, if they switched, not only would customers get a better product or service, but they would also save money. A no-brainer, right? Nope.

Without fail they haven't understood what their client really wants. On paper, it is irrational, but you have to embrace this irrationality and it starts with understanding what they want, so find out what matters to them and package it that way.

In the business of:
Save time, money ✓
and effort.

Do you really know what business you're in?

> "People don't want a quarter-inch drill –
> they want a quarter-inch hole."
> **Theodore Levitt**

When trying to identify what your consumers really want, it helps to start by identifying the business you are in, it might not be what you think. Most people think that they're in the business of selling widgets, or offering widget services, but that's not the business they are in at all. If you have a store that sells beautiful, artisan chocolates, what business are you in? If you sell lipstick, what business are you in? Hint - it's not the chocolate or the lipstick business.

It's not about what you sell, it's about why people buy what you sell. Making this shift is fundamental. To answer the above question, the chocolate shop is in the gift-giving business and realising this has a profound impact on how to run that business. It changes the way the business approaches customer loyalty as well as how it identifies joint venture partners and marketing channels, by exploring opportunities it wouldn't previously have thought of if it believed it was just in the chocolate business.

There is a famous quote that best explains the business the lipstick manufacturer is in:

"In the factory we make cosmetics; in the drugstore we sell hope"

Those are the words of Charles Revson, who launched Revlon back in the 1930's. He knew why women bought Revlon's products and, as a result, died a billionaire in 1975.

Not knowing what business you're in can be an easy mistake to make. What business do you think cinemas are in? It's not the movie business. The movie is the marketing hook, but the real profit comes from the popcorn, sweets and drinks. As you enter a cinema, the tantalising smell of popcorn is not an accident. Cinemas are in the fast-food business. Think about how they have increased their food offerings in the last few years to include pizzas, cheesy nacho's, even burritos.

ACTION

Get clear on the business you are in. Ask yourself the following questions:

☑ Why do your consumers come to you? What problem are they trying to solve?

☑ When they buy, who are they buying for?

☑ Which part of your business delivers the greatest profit margins?

☐? If your company folded tomorrow, where would your customers go?

TME

Family

wipes!

nothing on the market like it.

Marker: Parenting
Profitable niche
Potty Training

How to avoid marketing suicide

> "Be sure you positively identify your target
> before you pull the trigger."
> **Tom Flynn**

YOU'RE A NEEDLE AND YOUR MARKET IS A HAYSTACK

No matter what your product or service is or does, it is not suitable for everyone. Period! Targeting the mass market is marketing suicide. Even if you have a budget of billions of pounds, it's still a bad idea. If you really want to be successful, you need to start by identifying a profitable niche. By definition, it is less competitive, so it costs less to compete. Start by focusing on one niche and highlighting one benefit. I already know you have multiple benefits, but don't dilute your communications by throwing a whole list of features and benefits into every piece of communication, as they just get lost and serve only to confuse. You need to identify the main reason that your niche will buy your product or services. What is the one thing that makes your product or service irresistible to that niche? If you don't know what this is, then skip to "How to research buying behaviour" and discover how to find this out. You need to get comfortable with being single-minded, as it is much more effective at delivering results.

Fast, efficient and effective

a complete solution

> **Characteristics of profitable niches**
>
> When deciding on your niche, to be profitable, it needs to have the following characteristics:
>
> ☐ **Quantifiable:** Can you measure the size, purchasing power and key characteristics of the group? Ideally you want this niche to be growing.
>
> ☐ **Significant in size:** If the niche is too small it will not be a profitable target.
>
> ☐ **Easy to engage:** Can you communicate with it easily?
>
> ☐ **Differentiated:** Does this niche have relevant, distinguishing factors that mean, compared to other niches, it will respond differently to your communications?

Yes

Yes

Yes

Yes

need to understand this ✱

Once your product or service is selling successfully to one profitable niche, you can start to identify additional niches, but don't try and target too many when you start out. Are you familiar with Pareto's rule? In 1906, an Italian named Pareto identified that 80% of the land in Italy was owned by 20% of the people. This formula is one that has been applied to many situations with similar observations and is today referred to as Pareto's Rule; 20% of something is usually responsible for 80% of the results. If you start targeting multiple niches, you will soon notice this. If you're already established, take a look at your own business and see if 20% of your customers are delivering 80% of the profits. Don't waste those profits chasing unprofitable niches.

Similarly, If you have multiple products or services, analyse whether 20% of your portfolio are delivering 80% of your profits. If this is the case, then delist those that are draining your resources and not driving enough profit. It is important to be ruthless.

LOYALTY VERSUS PROFITABILITY

It's likely that your cost to acquire, serve and retain a consumer in each niche is more or less the same. You can therefore waste a lot of money focusing on niches that generate very little profit. Loyalty and profitability are very different and should not be confused – focus on retaining customers who are actually making you money, not costing you!

ACTIONS

Check that your target niche market meets the criteria for a profitable niche:

- ❏ Can you measure the size?
- ❏ Is it big enough?
- ❏ Is it easy to reach?
- ❏ Does it have a clear and unique need that makes your products or services relevant?

Conduct the 80:20 test on your business:

- ❏ Are 20% of your customers creating 80% of your revenue?
- ❏ Analyse the profitability of each niche and stop focusing on any that are unprofitable, instead put greater resources behind the most profitable.
- ❏ Are 20% of your products and services creating 80% of your profit?

Differentiate or die

> "Disruption is all about risk-taking, trusting your intuition, and rejecting the way things are supposed to be. Disruption goes way beyond advertising, it forces you to think about where you want your brand to go and how to get there."
>
> **Richard Branson**

Bland is boring. It blends in. It goes unnoticed and it is definitely not sought after. Daring to be different revolutionises business. However, 'different' needs to be significantly better and desirable. A marginal improvement is not going to blast you into the stratosphere, so let's set your expectations. Being exceptional matters, so find ways to stand out and be different. Forget about what they told you at school and find ways to be disruptive if you want your brand to stand out.

HOW CAN YOU SET YOURSELF APART?

When launching into any market, look for ways that you can disrupt the industry. What are the conventions of your category? A convention is something that is expected as it is offered by all of the key players. The fact that most household devices are turned on by switches is a convention, this was disrupted when clap technology was invented and devices could be turned on and off by the clap of hands. Dyson, the inventor, is a genius at breaking conventions through genuine product innovation; the blade-less fan and bag-less Hoover are two great category disruptions.

There are five different types of conventions that surround a category and the one that works for you might well be driven by budget limitations or simply the opportunity within your market. Let's explore each in turn.

1. **Performance:** What your product or service does
2. **Channel:** Where and how your product or services are offered
3. **Image:** How you present your brand
4. **Experience:** How people consume your brand
5. **Connection:** Whom you connect and partner with

not only offering a product
we offer education too

✓ **1. Performance Conventions**

These are conventions that govern what every product does and going beyond the basics can disrupt them. Dyson's bladeless fans cool you down, a tick for the basics, but they do so in a much smoother and altogether more impressive way than any other fans on the market, as they don't chop up the air before it hits you; a genuine disruption. Bose headphones aren't just comfortable and capable of delivering quality sound, they also offer the most effective noise cancelling solution on the market. Back at the start of the millennium, Honda wanted to create a better diesel engine, so they asked their chief designer, Kenichi Nagahiro, to design the company's first diesel engine, but he flatly refused. Nagahiro detested the noise, smell, and appearance of diesel engines. When asked if he could ever love a diesel engine, he replied that he could, if he were allowed to start completely from scratch. Nagahiro then designed the smoothest, most refined, least "'dieselly" diesel on the market. Wieden & ✳ Kennedy, Honda's advertising agency, then created one of the most awarded television campaigns to support the launch. The *needs* campaign was both a critical and financial success, as sales of *to be* diesel-engine Accords shot from 518 units in 2003 to 21,766 *done* units in 2004.

"Grrr" was part of the "Power of Dreams" campaign and you can view the ads here: www.jacquelinebiggs.com/honda

In the small business world, Glide is a great example of a company successfully challenging performance conventions in its

my sector

sector. Traditionally, in a student or multi-occupancy home, household bills are put in one or two people's names, their due dates are all at different times and invariably the person named on the bill is forced to chase late payers to get the bill paid on time. Glide has made bill paying simple by creating a platform that bundles all household services together and offers its customers the ability to divide up bills equally between residents with agreed monthly direct debit payments from each person. Glide therefore controls the bill payments and is responsible for chasing up late payers. This is ideal for students and tenants in multiple occupancy properties and it also works for business owners sharing an office space. Glide has grown to over 20,000 customers in just a few years, proving that the challenging of conventions really can pay off.

2. Channel Conventions

These govern where and how your products or services are offered; your distribution channels. The "route to consumer" is a key challenge facing many business to consumer brands today, as retailers are growing in power and squeezing the life out of brands by forcing aggressive promotions and price cuts. When challenging channel conventions, new distribution outlets need to fit with your brand by reaching the right target audience, reinforce your brand values and ideally surprise and delight your target audience. A unique and more convenient location can do great things for your brand, but it might only offer a brief first mover's advantage, as the competition can quickly follow suit. Pop-up restaurants, bars and shops that spring-up in unexpected locations were once the epitome of cool. They caused a storm and disappeared just before the fashion pack moved on to the next cool thing. Comme des Garçons started the trend in 2004 with its guerrilla stores, but now eight years on, London is literally pop-up-tastic with clothing stores, bars, restaurants and even office space springing up for short periods of time all over the city.

*look for what I am able to attach myself to

Whilst pop-up stores create a new channel, another option is to leverage an existing, but untapped distribution channel. Here are three examples of companies exploring new distribution channels, note that they each provide a "win-win" opportunity for both parties:

Whilst at a conference in a central London hotel the other day, I noticed that a company had installed a coin-operated phone-charger vending machine, ideal for conference attendees with flat batteries, as well as city break tourists who had left their chargers at home.

I ran in London's Nike 10k event a few years ago and once I had crossed the finish line, I was told I could go to the massage tent for a free massage. I was delighted. This was a great opportunity for local masseurs to demonstrate their abilities and to promote their services at the same time. I was so impressed with the masseur who looked after me, I booked regular massages with him for the next two years.

A few years ago Starbucks started featuring local artists in their stores, offering a new route to market for talented locals. This was a great opportunity for local artists, as Starbucks stores are always positioned in high footfall locations meaning more eyeballs on their work. It was also beneficial for Starbucks, as it helped to soften their corporate image and integrated them more into the local community.

3. Image Conventions

These surround how you present yourself; the visual side of your branding. In beer commercials there is always a pint shown, beaded in condensation to drive "thirst-appeal". Most shampoo ads have someone shaking out a long, glossy mane of hair. Make-up brands often have a famous face representing their brand. When it comes to packaging; eggs usually come in cardboard cartons, water is sold in clear bottles, sportswear brands associate with professional athletes. There are myriad image conventions

that govern different categories and breaking with these can
make your brand stand out. *Animal Themed*

Innocent challenged image conventions when it launched, with
its "chatty" packaging designed to create an emotional connection with the consumer. Why should packaging just display
functional information? Why not change it frequently? Innocent founders wanted to make their brand feel human and not
a faceless behemoth. Encouraging people to visit them at Fruit
Towers, or to call them on the banana phone made them feel
approachable and friendly. Rather than having traditional delivery vans they created "Dancing Grass Vans" and "Cow Vans",
complete with horns, eyelashes, udders and a tail and a button
that made them go "Moo". Their consistent tone of voice across
every possible channel helped to create the phenomenal brand
that is Innocent.

If you run a local sandwich shop, instead of wrapping sand-
wiches in a traditional plain white paper bag, why not make it
say something about your brand? If you are a hairdresser why
not take a photo of your clients as they leave your salon looking
amazing and send it to them when they are due for an appoint-
ment to remind them just how great you can make them look.
If you're a painter or decorator, don't just put your business card
through someone's door, be creative, perhaps put your contact
information on the back of a postcard of a beautiful piece of
art, people are much more likely to pin it to their fridge and to
remember you for doing something different.

4. Experience Conventions

These govern how consumers experience your brand and range
from live events through to how your product or service is consumed. People love to share their experiences so creating one
worth talking about can do wonders for your brand.

The launch of Magner's Original Irish cider in the UK a few
years ago was quite a sensation, as it introduced drinkers to the
concept of drinking cider in a pint glass, rammed with ice. A

whole new experience. This created great bar theatre and the trend quickly took hold creating an extraordinary revival of cider.

Nintendo's launch of Wii completely revolutionised the gaming market as it radically changed how games were played. Traditionally, playing a game created little movement beyond the furious button pressing of consoles. Wii introduced a radical new concept that got players up and out of their seats and physically involved in the games they were playing. Players moved from simply playing, to experiencing the action for themselves. Critically it took the gamer out of the bedroom and into the lounge as the appeal of the Wii was widespread and involved the whole family in the fun experience.

I worked with a small hairdressing chain to help them to increase customer loyalty. I spent a couple of days just watching how they treated their customers from the point they entered the store to when they left. It was like a conveyor belt; they were overlapping appointments, starting lots of clients late and always chasing their tails and apologising. They saw their clients as numbers and knew they needed to get a certain number in each chair each day to be profitable. They had totally forgotten about the customer's experience, which is why the percentage of returning clients had dropped off a cliff. When I took them through my observations they were mortified. I ran a series of short interviews with their existing customers to explore what they could do to improve their experience. The changes were simple, but made a big difference. Their customers loved getting their hair cut, it was time out from their life and a moment of relaxation. They just wanted to feel special whilst they were at the salon, not rushed in and rushed out and importantly they were willing to pay for a more indulgent experience. So, instead of coming in to just get a hair cut, we created pamper sessions which included a glass of wine, a cappuccino or a herbal tea, a head massage and a foot spa. Their clients loved it as they left feeling truly relaxed and whilst each client spent more time at the salon, which meant one less client per chair per day, the increased prices that customers were willing to pay for the experience meant profits were up too. More importantly it increased client retention and generated word of mouth resulting in more clients.

5. Connection Conventions

This governs with whom you partner and connect to co-create your product or service. Surprising pairings can create a lot of interest in your brand. In the last few years a number of up-market designers have partnered with retailers at the lower end of the fashion market, but with great success. Designers are keen to appeal to the masses and have created bespoke lines with mass-market appeal (and prices) and they have flown out of the store. H&M has run joint ventures with Karl Lagerfeld, Stella McCartney, Viktor and Rolf, Madonna, Roberto Cavalli and Matthew Williamson to name but a few. Marks and Spencer collaborated with Conrans; George at Asda with Max Azria. Many people who had never been into these stores flocked in droves to get their hands on the designer lines.

If you run a cafe, bar or restaurant that has a local celebrity client, why not ask them what their favourite cake, sandwich, bottle of wine, or cocktail is and add their endorsement to your menu, or create something special with their name on. Even if they don't come in, but they do live locally, find the name of their agent through Google and contact them with your suggestion. It works.

BREAKING CONVENTIONS

It's important to give potential customers a compelling reason to choose you over your competitors, but finding that reason is not always easy. Start by talking to your target audience about what they love and hate about your competitors, ask them what improvements they would like to see in your sector, you never know what you might uncover. Any challenge needs to be grounded in a strong insight into what your consumer really wants or thinks, so how you break the convention links directly to this. Your objective is to change the rules of the category so they play to your favour. *Yes I know this*.

It's useful to look at unrelated categories. How have new players into the market successfully challenged the status quo and what can you learn from them? What's your equivalent to Apple's genius bar? Virgin took on all the other airlines by doing things differently, a bar on the plane, television screens in the back of the seats, chauffeurs to take you from your home to check-in. David can take on Goliath and win. You need to understand what consumers want and then give it to them. Exploratory questions enable you to challenge conventions. Successful brands ask why not? They don't rule out possibilities, they embrace them and see where they can take them. Today's conventions do not have to be tomorrow's.

GET INSPIRED

It's useful to look at successful, disruptive brands in non-related sectors to see what you can learn from them. It's a great way to get inspired and challenge the way you view your industry. When thinking about how to disrupt a category, deconstruct the strategies of some of the most successful brands.

- ☑ **Red Bull** is one of the most famous disruptive brands, as its arrival created not just a new brand but a whole new category: the energy drink.

- ☑ **Skype** disrupted the telecom industry as the first brand to deliver high quality talk and conference facilities over the Internet at low prices.

- ☐ **Zynga**, most famous for CityVille, FarmVille and Mafia Wars, turned the video gaming market on its head with the launch of social gaming

- ☐ **Zara** is unlike traditional clothes retailers, as it directly manages the whole cycle "from the notepad sketch to the clothes hanger" enabling it to disrupt the time it takes to get from catwalk to store

- **Innocent** disrupted the role of packaging and used it as a key communication channel rather than a functional form - this enabled them to engage with consumers on a whole new level.

- **Virgin** disrupts every category it enters - in fact Branson only enters markets he knows he can disrupt

- **Pringles** disrupted packaging conventions by launching a cylindrical form instead of the category norm of bags.

- **EasyJet** and Ryanair disrupted the airline market with their no-frills offering

---

Vive la révolution!

Apple's iPod revolutionised the mp3 sector. It irrevocably altered our buying, listening and viewing habits more than any of its rivals. Apple created a cult must-have product that millions of people can't live without. We can buy songs in the comfort of our own home thanks to iTunes, Apple's online music store. We can listen to podcasts, watch episodes of our favourite TV shows on the bus to school or work, some companies even use them for staff training, requiring employees to download relevant training materials to their device. We can even use them as remote controls.

Not only have iPods changed our social and working lives, they have revolutionised the way that artists and record labels make and sell music. In addition TV and film companies now sell through iTunes and produce special recordings for free download. Audio books are another huge sales segment, revolutionising the publishing industry.

With sales reaching over $3 billion a year, it's fair to say that the iPod challenged the status quo and improved the way that we consume music, TV and books.

ACTION

Think about how you could be the only one who does what you do, seek scarcity and you will reap the rewards. Think about how you can challenge conventional thinking. What can you do differently? Go through each convention and brainstorm how you could disrupt your market. To get started, answer the following questions:

❑ **Performance:** How could you improve your products or services? What could you simplify or streamline? What could you do more, or less of?

❑ **Channel:** Who has the power in your distribution strategy? If it's not you, what could you do to reverse this? Could you find a joint venture partner and together create a new route to market? Where could you offer your product or service that would surprise and delight your target? Could you take your products or services to your consumers rather than them coming to you?

❑ **Image:** List all the image conventions that govern your market, think about the codes and cues that exist in all forms of marketing from packaging to advertising. What could you change, tweak or adapt to shake up your market?

❑ **Experience:** Take a look at how and where your product or service is consumed. What could you do to create more theatre or a greater experience? Could you move what is traditionally indoors, outdoors? Does the temperature play a role in your customers' experience? Could you lower it like London's Ice Bar, or increase it like Hot Bikram Yoga?

❑ **Connection:** With what other brands could you co-create products or services to increase demand?

CREATING A BRAND STRATEGY

What is a brand anyway?

"A brand for a company is like a reputation
for a person. You earn reputation by trying
to do hard things well."
Jeff Bezos

When defining what a brand is I find it helps to start with what a brand is not. It isn't a logo. It isn't a consistent brand look and feel on everything from your website to your stationery. It isn't a product. It's not what you say it is either. A brand doesn't really exist. It exists only in the minds of your consumers. It is everything they know, think and feel about your products or services. A brand is also a promise and it's vital that this promise is kept.

When creating a brand it's important to be consistent inside the company and out. A strong mission and sense of purpose are powerful ways to create internal consistency. For many companies, the founder drives this sense of clarity and purpose and the brand reflects their view of the world.

GET ON A MISSION

Every company needs a mission to set them on the path to greatness. A mission statement outlines your company's purpose; it defines what drives you and reveals your passions. Your mission is about the meaning behind the money. Companies that live and breathe their passions and are the same on the inside as they are on the outside, are companies that people trust and with which they can connect. Your mission therefore drives the day-to-day running of your business from top to bottom. Every member of your staff should know your company mission, which creates unity and focus as everyone working on the brand feels like they're part of a big movement.

Case Study: Zappos

Zappos is an American online retailer selling shoes and clothing. Nick Swinmurn founded Zappos in 1999, because he couldn't find the shoes he wanted at a San Francisco shopping mall. When he got home he tried online, but without success. On the spur of the moment, he decided to quit his job and start an online retailer. The company needed funding and one of the investors was Tony Hsieh who, a few months after launch, decided that selling shoes was more fun than being an investor and joined as CEO. Tony successfully doubled Zappos revenues every year, starting with $1.6 million in 2000. By 2009, revenues reached $1 billion. So how did he do it?

It is all down to their unique mission that permeates every single element of the company.

Zappos Mission: To provide the best customer service possible. Internally, we call this our WOW philosophy.

Zappos don't sell shoes and clothes, they sell happiness. They wanted their brand to be focused on delivering the "very best customer service and the very best customer experience". They believe that customer service shouldn't be just a department, it should be the entire company. To deliver what they call their "wow" service, they ensure items get delivered to customers as quickly as possible. To do this, the company invests in warehouses and everything they sell they ship themselves, unlike most other online retailers. The process costs more, but they have total control over the customer experience. Tony also believes that by being good to his employees – for example by paying 100 per-cent of their health care premiums, spending heavily on personal development, and giving customer service representatives more freedom than at a typical call centre – they would be able to offer better service than their competitors. They even pay new employees $2,000 to quit if they're unhappy with their jobs! Hiring the right people is critical to their business, so they put every employee through two sets of interviews, one that assesses their fit with the team, their experience, technical ability etc and the second assesses their cultural fit. Candidates have to pass both to be hired. All new employees, whether senior management or a graduate, then go through a four week training on the company culture, company history, their approach to customer service, followed by two weeks taking customer calls. Their goal is to deliver 100% excellent service, as better service translates into lots of repeat customers, which has meant long-term profits, low marketing expenses and fast growth.

Zappos wanted to build their brand, not through advertising, which is notoriously difficult in today's market, but through culture. They believe that "if you get the culture right, most of the other stuff -- like great customer service, or building a great long-term brand, or passionate employees and customers -- will happen naturally on its own." Their culture is so strong that they have put together a dictionary of Zappos-invented words. They have zuddles in the call centres (huddles), they earn zollars for great work and they can redeem these in a company store. Wow is of course their big one.

Today brands are built on the domino effect of personal recommendations. If, like Zappos, you focus on delivering a wow experience every time, then you set yourself up for success.

So your mission isn't about *what* you sell, it's about *why* you sell. A national chain of bicycle shops doesn't just sell bikes, its mission is to reduce the UK's carbon footprint. A local cafe sells healthy lunches but their mission is to give busy executives one healthy food choice a day. Here are a few missions from some well-known brands to inspire you to create your own:

Nike's Mission: To bring inspiration and innovation to every athlete[4] in the world.

---

4   *"If you have a body, you are an athlete."* Bill Bowerman

Google's Mission: To organise the world's information and make it universally accessible and useful.

Coca-Cola's Mission: To refresh the world...

Microsoft's Mission: To put a computer on every desk in every home.

SUMMARY

Your mission outlines what you want to achieve by starting your company and from this flows your vision and values which we explore in the next chapter. Combined they can provide inspiration and momentum to your business.

ACTION

So what's your mission? Start by answering the following questions:

- ❑ What gets you out of bed in the morning?
- ❑ What gives your business a competitive edge?
- ❑ What's your passion? What inspires you?
- ❑ What do you stand for and how can you ensure it permeates everything that you do?

How to nail your vision and values

"A leader has the vision and conviction
that a dream can be achieved. He inspires
the power and energy to get it done."

Ralph Lauren

MISSION, VISION, VALUES - WHY DO THEY MATTER?

Your company's mission, vision and set of unique values are key to setting a clear direction for you, your partners, your staff, your investors and your customers. The more clearly you can articulate your high level goals at the start, the less time you will spend fixing cultural clashes later. This powerful trio also form the foundations of your brand story which is key to creating an emotional connection with your customers and your employees.

Strong brands are very clear about what they stand for and why they exist and this permeates everything that they do. Their identity is founded on a very strong product or brand truth that is unique, credible and hugely compelling. Importantly, they do not let the competition define them as they have identified a unique place in the market. At times the founder drives this vision and purpose and the brand story reflects his or her view of the world. Virgin reflects Richard Branson's personal beliefs, The Body Shop reflects the late Anita Roddick's, Apple reflects Steve Job's and Starbucks' reflects the personal beliefs of Howard Shultz. Each of these leaders is the living embodiment of the brand. What they do and how they behave sets the direction of the brand. They all have a very clear mission, vision and values and their passion for change comes through in their brand stories.

VISION

Your vision should be a rallying cry. It's what drives you forward, even when everything feels stacked against you and is a powerful motivator. It should describe an ideal future that reflects what your company represents, not just what it does. If it's vivid and meaningful, people can do incredible things to make it happen. Just look at Martin Luther King; he had an incredibly powerful vision that motivated many to get behind him to help it become a reality:

Martin Luther King: "I have a dream that my four little children will one day live in a nation where they will not be judged by the colour of their skin, but by the content of their character."

However, don't feel that you have to have a big vision, you might not want to change the world and that's fine. Global domination might not be your goal and that's fine too. What is important is that your vision is optimistic and motivating. It helps to put a timescale on your vision, which can be one, two or five years; there is no right way to decide on your timeframe, it is driven by you.

BRAND VALUES

These are a set of rules by which you and all your employees live (and work). These are the things you won't compromise on. Your brand values guide your behaviour like a code of honour, permeating every little thing that you do. They should be much more than just words on a page. Your company culture is what sets you apart. Your product or services or systems could all be copied, but your culture is inimitable.

Your values reveal not only who you are as an organisation, but also who you are not. They reflect your ethics, principles and beliefs about your company and its place in the world. They tend to be unchanging, usually remaining the same for the life of your company. As the founder, they are likely to be the same, or similar to your own, personal values.

When writing your values, keep the following in mind:

- ❏ Keep it simple, just one or two sentences for each value.

- ❏ Think about the effect you want your words to have on the reader - write to inspire.

- ❏ Think about the words you use carefully and avoid clichés - "Quality" and "Innovation" are overused and bland. Make yours memorable, inspiring and unique.

- ❏ Can each value help you to be distinctive?

- ❏ Is it relevant to your brand, to your consumers and to your staff?

- ❏ Can it be brought to life in behaviour? This is key, as you should hire and fire on values.

Here are some examples to inspire you into action. Note the relationship between the vision and values; the values help you to make the vision a reality.

BBC

Our vision: To be the most creative organisation in the world.

Our values:

- Trust is the foundation of the BBC: we are independent, impartial and honest.
- Audiences are at the heart of everything we do.
- We take pride in delivering quality and value for money.
- Creativity is the lifeblood of our organisation.
- We respect each other and celebrate our diversity so that everyone can give their best.
- We are one BBC: great things happen when we work together.

INNOCENT

Our vision: To be the earth's favourite little food company.

Our values: We have one core principle, around which we make all of our decisions:

Create a business we can be proud of

We then break this down into five values, each reflecting what we are, how we do things, and where we increasingly want to be:

- **Be natural.** We want to make 100% natural, delicious, healthy stuff, 100% of the time. For us, being natural is also about keeping it human and putting people first. We want to treat others, especially our drinkers, as we'd like to be treated ourselves.

- **Be entrepreneurial.** Innocent began as a small, entrepreneurial company, and nothing much has changed. We chase every opportunity and try to be as responsive as we can - to our consumers, our customers, and to opportunities in the market. We want to be creative and challenge the status quo. We want to do what we do better than anyone else, and have fun doing it.

- **Be commercial.** We are a commercial business and so creating growth and profit for us and our customers is central to what we do and why we are here. We need to be tough, but at the same time fair. We need to think clearly, act decisively and keep the main thing the main thing.

- **Be generous.** With our feedback for others, with our time when coaching others, with rewards when people deliver, and with our charitable support. It's that simple.

TESCO

Our vision: To create value for customers and earn their lifetime loyalty.

Our values: No one tries harder

- Understand customers.

- Be first to meet their needs.
- Act responsibly for our communities.

Treat people as we want to be treated

- Work as a team.
- Trust and respect each other.
- Listen, support and say thank you.
- Share knowledge and experience.
- ...So we can enjoy our work.

To illustrate how Tesco want their staff to live their vision and values, their brand team created a steering wheel with five segments, Community, Operations, People, Finance and Customer. They measure the performance of each of their businesses against this wheel to help to maintain focus and balance on what counts. Their vision permeates everything they do right through to their core brand promise that "every little helps".

You could create a visual word map for your value statements and share this with your team. Wordle.net is a free tool to help you do this.

SUMMARY

Getting clear on your mission, vision and value statements will help you to create a strong brand identity and a sense of community. It will help you to shape your culture, a key differentiator for your brand. It is important to stretch yourself, push your boundaries and create a culture that really stands out and draws people to you.

ACTION

Get each member of the management team to create vision and value statements, start by answering the following questions separately and compare and contrast.

Vision:

- ❑ What do you want to be remembered for five years from now?
- ❑ What do you want people to be saying about your brand?
- ❑ What impact do you want to have on society?

Values:

- ❏ What drives you?

- ❏ What type of behaviour is important to you?

- ❏ What do you love and what do you hate about the way people work together?

- ❏ What are the guiding principles that have got you where you are today?

- ❏ Is each value distinct, compelling and authentic?

- ❏ Can it be brought to life in behaviour?

Once completed, share these, together with your mission statement with a wider team for additional feedback.

What's your brand story?

"People will forget what you said, forget
what you did, but they will never forget
how you made them feel."
Maya Angelo

Hemingway was challenged to tell a story in six words and he
told this, the world's greatest short story:

For Sale: Baby shoes, never worn.

In just six words he tugs at our emotional heart strings and our
minds whir with sad possibilities. What a powerful copywriter.
What a powerful storyteller.

WHAT'S YOUR STORY?

Every brand has a story, but many never realise them or tell them
in an engaging way. A compelling brand narrative is something
people relate to, believe in and enjoy. If you want to stand the
test of time, you need to tell yours.

Your mission, vision and values are just one part of your brand
story. This bigger story is what connects your brand to your consumer and makes it relevant to their lives. You want to take your
audience on a journey with your brand. A great brand story is
authentic and creative. It enables you to connect emotionally
and personally with your consumer and inspires action. Dove
and Persil are two brands with great stories:

Dove's brand story

Dove has a big brand vision; they want to create a world where
beauty is a source of confidence, not anxiety. Dove believes that

every woman is beautiful which is why they want to help women and girls to free themselves from beauty stereotypes. They are on a mission to help women discover their true self confidence. This message is at the heart of their "Campaign for Real Beauty" that first launched back in 2004. The campaign celebrated the natural, physical differences of women and featured women of all shapes and sizes with love handles and cellulite to demonstrate that we should all learn to be confident in our own skin. You can see some of the ads here: www.jacquelinebiggs.com/Dove

In 2006, Dove started the Dove Self-Esteem Fund to continue its mission to try to change the way women and young girls perceive beauty. They are focused on shifting the concept of beauty from ultra-thin models with "perfect" features to making every girl (and woman) feel positive about her looks. The fact that to date they have reached over five million lives worldwide is a reflection of their powerful brand story, which compelled so many to connect with it.

Persil's brand story

Persil believes that "children should be given the freedom to be creative – which leads to their learning and development – without worrying about getting dirty." Their belief that "dirt is good" launched a global campaign that celebrated and encouraged children to get dirty. Embracing its nemesis, Persil's campaign explored the developmental benefits of getting dirty. Ads carried strap-lines such as "It's not mess, it's curiosity" and "It's not dirt, it's man of the match". You can see some of the campaign here: www.jacquelinebiggs.con/Persil. Finally there was a creative strategy in an incredibly bland category, where every brand promised to make your whites, whiter than white. By celebrating dirt and creating a great brand story about how every child has the right to be a child Persil aimed to connect with mums the world over.

Dove's Campaign for real beauty and Persil's desire to give kids the freedom to get dirty are two powerful brand stories. Their conviction and deep-seated beliefs are the starting point for a great story about their brands. They are brands with opinions and opinions create conversations. Importantly, both brand stories connect a brand's truth, values and beliefs with a strong insight into the target audience. This is what makes them both compelling and relevant. A great brand story enables you to connect emotionally with your consumers, which is the key to success.

STOP POLISHING THE PYRAMID

Whenever I have worked with FTSE 100 clients, we have always spent a lot of time discussing the meaning of their brands. What did they stand for? What was the core essence of the brand? The values? The personality? The emotional and rational benefits? Plus a lot more. Each client had a different way of setting out their brand architecture and it varied from pyramids to temples to onions and beyond.

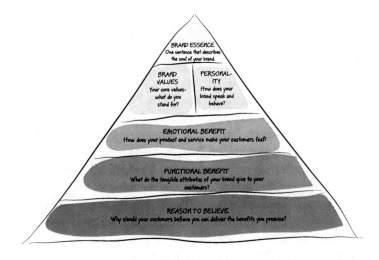

Oh how we agonised over the words. Was the brand smart or intelligent? Laid-back or relaxed? We spent weeks discussing nuances of synonyms and performed semantic gymnastics. Now, don't get me wrong, I actually do think that the discipline of articulating your brand pyramid or equivalent is a good one, but you have to make sure that it takes you to a useful place rather than leading to death by a hundred adjectives. I have always thought that storytelling is a much more effective way to bring a brand's intangible characteristics and values to life. Stories have the power to evoke intense emotions but, quite frankly, pyramids do not. If you think about brand development as the creation of a story that people want to listen to and be a part of, it can give real meaning to that collection of adjectives.

THE ART OF STORYTELLING

The most powerful content tells a story. We've all been touched by stories since our childhood, which both entertain and enrich us. If you reflect on myths and famous childhood stories, you will notice that common themes recur across cultures, as well as in our own lives. The same common themes occur in films and in books, that reflect our experiences in dealing with the human condition and form the basis of how we make sense of the world, which is why we connect with them. It's not always conscious, but subconsciously it drives a lot of what we do and how we think.

To succeed, brands need to connect with consumers with emotion and relevance; the application of storytelling principles to brand development strategy can make that journey more effective. A brand is a metaphorical story and the most compelling stories are often woven around a central character or personality. So when creating your story it helps to consider which archetype best fits your brand. Archetypes were introduced by Carl Jung, a Swiss psychiatrist, who used them to explain how subconscious perceptions are created by certain symbols and images. In Jungian psychology, an archetype is a collectively inherited unconscious idea, pattern of thought or image that is universally present in individual psyches. So, if I say "lover", a certain image comes straight to your mind; a very different image and set of perceptions come to mind if I then say "mother". Exploring archetypes in your brand development process is a great way to tap into and create the identity of your brand. If I describe the Virgin brand by saying it's "Robin Hood, the people's champion", this evokes a rich tapestry of emotions and connections and is significantly more emotive than saying "Virgin challenges the status quo".

Weaving your story around an archetype can help you to create an immediate and strong emotional connection with your consumers as archetypes are, by definition, hugely emotive; so why not build your brand on values that have been in existence for hundreds, or even thousands of years?

THE TWELVE MASTER CHARACTER ARCHETYPES

We all have hard-wired archetypal patterns that manifest themselves at different times in different ways and at a constant level, with one being more dominant depending on our personality type. Think about your peers and friendship groups and you find the Rebel, the Explorer and, the salt of the earth, Regular Guy. At times I am sure that you have felt protective or competitive and maybe even campaigned for justice; what you might not have realised is that these are all archetypes, basic patterns of behaviour. Every archetype has its own set of values, ambitions and behaviour and this helps us to realise our own unconscious ambitions and aspirations. They are very powerful drivers of our behaviour.

Inspired by the work of Pearson (1991), I am going to introduce you to twelve archetypes that have stood the test of time. This is not an exhaustive list – as Jung himself said, there can be many, many archetypes – but these are the most common and a great starting point. The intention is not to pigeon hole your brand into one of the twelve archetypes, as this is not a "cookie cutter" approach. Each archetype has a set of sub identities that enable you to tailor your identity to your unique brand. Exploring and defining the sub-identities is where the fun begins and at Brand Camp we have created a process – *The Brand Archetype Blueprint* – that helps you to create your unique brand identity. This process begins with identifying your dominant archetype from the twelve master archetypes and then selecting one or two sub-identities. It's important to view your brand in a competitive context, so as you go through the archetypes consider which best suit your competitors, as you need to create an emotionally distinct positioning.

The Innocent

Innocent individuals want to create peace, harmony and happiness in the world. Their strong set of values and beliefs drive everything they do. As natural optimists they don't take no for an answer and they tenaciously focus on achieving their lofty goals. They are hugely motivated and soldier on, breaking down barriers that others struggle with.

- **Motto:** Do what's right
- **Sub-identities:** Angel, Child, Philanthropist
- **Brands:** Innocent, Dove

The Regular Guy

Everyman individuals are kind, responsible, decent and all round nice guys. They get on with everyone and love to be depended on and needed. Not only do they have a need to belong, but they are great at bringing people together as they are great team players, loyal to the end.

- **Motto:** Never let anyone down
- **Sub-identities:** Best friend, Sympathiser, Egalitarian
- **Brands:** Tesco, Gillette

The Explorer

Explorer individuals are happiest when they are exploring new territories and possibilities. They are independent and naturally curious and they love helping people to find out who they are by exploring the world.

- **Motto:** To blaze a new trail
- **Sub-identities:** Maverick, Thrill-seeker, Pioneer
- **Brands:** Jeep, North Face

The Caregiver

Caregiver individuals love to do things for other people and their compassion and generosity knows no bounds. They love to support others in times of need and are great at motivating others to improve the service of care that they provide.

- **Motto:** Protect and care for others

- **Sub-identities:** Nurse, Mother, Helper

- **Brands:** Red Cross, Pampers

The Hero

Hero individuals love to take on challenges and the bigger the better. They are courageous individuals, driven by a desire to win as they want to have a major impact on the world. They are great at motivating others to achieve their goals as their courage, determination and perseverance are infectious.

- **Motto:** Fight for our rights

- **Sub-identities:** Daredevil, Activist, Opportunist

- **Brands:** Virgin, The British Army

The Ruler

Ruler individuals are work-a-holics. They were born to lead and are tough, decisive and goal-orientated. They love to be in control and are great organisers of people. They are very successful at creating a prosperous community and experts at creating order from chaos.

- **Motto:** Take charge
- **Sub-identities:** King, Dictator, Tycoon
- **Brands:** Microsoft, Goldman Sachs

The Jester

Jester individuals live in the moment and focus on having a good time and lightening up the world. They don't take life too seriously and are naturally playful and spontaneous. They love to help people see the funny side of situations and are experts at defusing stressful situations.

- **Motto:** You only live once
- **Sub-identities:** Clown, Self deprecator, Satirist
- **Brands:** Foster's, Ben & Jerry's

The Magician

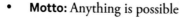

Magician individuals' greatest talent lies in their ability to make things happen. They create a vision and see it through. They are insightful and inspiring and great at empowering teams. They have a unique ability to turn problems into opportunities and tirelessly focus on creating win-win outcomes at all times.

- **Motto:** Anything is possible
- **Sub-identities:** Prophet, Charmer, Illusionist
- **Brands:** Peace One Day, Glastonbury Festival

The Creator

Creator individuals love to create things of enduring value. They are incredibly creative and visionary with a limitless imagination. Their talent lies in their ability to inspire creativity in others and they get very excited about the chance to demonstrate their original thinking.

- **Motto:** If you can imagine it, it can be done
- **Sub-identities:** Expert, Architect, Author
- **Brands:** Dyson, Lego

The Sage

Sage individuals use intelligence and analysis to understand the world. They are information hungry and always seeking new information to help them make sense of a problem or challenge. They are logical thinkers that love to self reflect and carefully form their opinions. Their expertise lies in helping to make the complex simple and they motivate others to seek the truth.

- **Motto:** The truth will set you free
- **Sub-identities:** Scholar, Prodigy, Authority
- **Brands:** Google, Reuters

The Lover

Lover individuals fear being alone and crave intimacy. They are happiest when they surround themselves with the people they love as they enjoy building relationships. They are passionate and committed and want to please others. They dislike cliques and a "them and us" attitude, so they are experts at bringing people together.

- **Motto:** I only have eyes for you
- **Sub-identities:** Temptress, Libertine, Virgin
- **Brands:** Haagen Dazs, Godiva

The Rebel

Rebel individuals love to challenge the status quo and overturn what isn't working. They like to shock and disrupt and pave the way for revolutionary new attitudes. They love to motivate others to think differently and they're capable of developing groundbreaking new approaches.

- **Motto:** Rules are made to be broken

- **Sub-identities:** Revolutionary, Champion, Radical

- **Brands:** Harley-Davidson, Honda

Some brands fit squarely into one archetype, but for others, a second can be present, though less dominant. The uniqueness of your brand is then brought out by the selection of sub-identities and this requires a lot of thought and exploration with both your team and your target market. It's a hugely beneficial exercise as brands with strong identities, like Apple, Nike and IKEA have a large and loyal following, as people connect to their strong beliefs and consistent values. I haven't detailed information on each of the sub-identities mentioned but if you would like to delve into this further I have put additional information on the website. www.jacquelinebiggs.com/archetypes

ACTION

❏ You need to ensure that your brand identity is sufficiently differentiated from your competition, but before you assign an archetype to your brand, brainstorm what defines the uniqueness of your brand. Capture key words and phrases, as these will help you to select your archetypes.

❏ List out the key players in your category and assign a primary archetype to each, including your brand.

❏ Next think about which sub identities best fit with your brand, you can find out more information on the website detailed above.

❏ Once you're happy with your selection it's time to craft your brand story. (See next chapter)

How to tell your story

> "Those who do not have power over the story that dominates their lives, the power to retell it, rethink it, deconstruct it, joke about it, and change it as times change, truly are powerless, because they cannot think new thoughts."
>
> **Salman Rushdie**

STRONG BRAND STORIES

Once you have identified your brand archetypes, you then need to craft your brand story. This could be about how you began, what makes you different or what and why you do what you do. The best brand stories are irresistible and compelling. They tell the unexpected and speak directly to the heart. Whether word of mouth or online, the ancient art of storytelling remains the same. It's the passion, the creativity, and the integrity of the message that makes a story powerful. And powerful stories change the world.

WHY IS STORYTELLING SO IMPORTANT TO YOUR BUSINESS?

- ☑ An authentic brand story makes you memorable.
- ☑ It differentiates you as desirable.
- ☑ It reveals how you solve a genuine problem.
- ☑ It solidifies your culture.
- ☑ It brings your brand to life and makes you feel human.
- ☑ It gives you a distinct competitive advantage.
- ☑ Your target market becomes hugely responsive - good stories drive the audience to action.
- ☑ It can position you as a visionary in your field.

HOW DO YOU BEGIN FRAMING YOUR OWN BRAND STORY?

An effective brand story is authentic and creative, it has the same components that you see in a novel you can't put down, or a film you watch a hundred times. It emotionally engages the audience, touching them in a personal way. It's the opposite of a "hard sell", instead you take people on a powerful journey with your brand. Great brand stories reveal the human side to a brand and get the audience to take action, whether it's to think or feel differently about something, to change their behaviour or to spend money. In short, great brand stories compel people to action.

When crafting your story begin with the end in mind - what do you want your consumers to think, feel or do on hearing your brand story? Then think about how you are going to measure this. There is no point in crafting an incredible piece of communication if you cannot track its effectiveness. Ideally you want to create a story that starts a conversation.

Once you understand the impact you want to have, try answering some of the following questions to help you identify your brand story. The work you have already done on your mission, vision and value statements will drive a lot of your responses:

1. What motivated and inspired you to start your company?

2. What's your mission? What makes life meaningful for you?

3. What are the attitudes and beliefs that shape your business culture?

4. What makes you stand out from the crowded market place?

5. How do your products and services meet your consumers' emotional needs?

6. What problem are you solving?

7. What is the single, most important message that you want to convey?

8. What do you want people to think, feel or do on hearing or reading your story?

THE MEDIUM AFFECTS THE MESSAGE

How will you tell your story? Through video or the written word? Where will you share it? On your website, your blog, across social media, via a third party? How you tell the story will differ depending on the channel it is told through, so consider where your target audience will be when they are exposed to your message; consider their emotional state when they engage with the media. This will help you to hone how you tell the story across channels. That said, no matter where the message is delivered, you need to tell a consistent story. Inconsistencies dilute a message and confuse, but worst of all they create distrust.

ACTION

❑ Start planning your brand story by answering the 8 questions above.

❑ Next, set the scene; define the key players and agree on the key message that will be consistently communicated across channels.

❑ Decide which channels to use to tell your story and think about the different role for communication for each. For example, the role for your blog could be to educate and update people about your mission, whilst the role for Facebook is to inspire people to share your story.

❑ Ensure that your story is distinctive and has clear benefits for your target market.

Quantity or quality?

> "A good decision is based on knowledge
> and not on numbers."
> **Plato**

QUANTITY DOES NOT MATTER

Some people subscribe to the theory that marketing is all about quantity - if you hit a large enough pool of people, some of them will always buy. Well, yes, this is true, but what a waste of time, money and other resources. What really counts is the quality of the people you connect with, as you want the conversion rate of prospects to customers to be high. For example, if you sell golfing holidays, running an ad in Golfer's Weekly would be much more effective than an ad in a national paper. The golfing magazine guarantees a pre qualified audience of golf lovers. They still might not be interested in your golfing holiday, but we'll come to that.

STRANGERS VS PROSPECTS

The dictionary definition of a stranger is "a person unaccustomed or unacquainted with something", in this instance, your products or services. On the other hand, a prospect is "a potential, or likely customer or client". Prospects are therefore infinitely more valuable than strangers, as they are pre-qualified, they have already shown an interest in what you have to offer, so the chance of converting them is much higher. Unfortunately, a lot of people waste far too much time chasing strangers with a scatter gun strategy. So how do you find these high quality prospects and how do you go about converting them?

WAYS TO FIND AND CONVERT HIGH QUALITY PROSPECTS

Set up a referral network

What companies target the same niche as you in a non competitive way? Call them up and ask them if they would be interested in offering your products and services to their clients and customers on a revenue share basis. You can then return the favour and promote their goods and services to your customer base. If you are a physiotherapist then referring business to complementary practitioners, such as acupuncturists, can be a great source of qualified leads. If you run a veterinary practice, you could set up a referral scheme with the local cattery, dogs' home or stables. If you are a photographer and take corporate head shots, you could ask business coaches and trainers to refer business to you. Electricians and plumbers can easily refer clients to each other. The list goes on. Think about the type of companies that would benefit from referring their clients and customers to your business. (For more ideas on how to set up joint venture opportunities see the chapter, "Customer acquisition strategies".

Competing Business

Approach direct competitors and ask if they will sell you unconverted leads or lapsed customers. In tough times many companies would rather guarantee a revenue stream than miss out. If competing businesses are going through tough times, you might even consider offering to buy this part of their business if it is an area of strength for you.

Build your own list

Without doubt, this is the most effective strategy, it does take time and effort, but you can potentially reap the rewards for years to come. Social media is key to list building and in the chapters, "How to create a social media strategy" and "How to build a subscriber list" I outline how to do this in detail, but here are some of the ideas.

SOCIAL MEDIA LIST BUILDING STRATEGIES

When it comes to social media, it is important to think strategically about where your target audience is most likely to spend their time online. It's important to go beyond Facebook and Twitter and focus on super targeted locations where a conversation about your products or service is already happening. Let's take a look at these.

Targeted articles and blogs

Google offers a free keyword tool that indicates how many searches there are each month on any combination of keywords. Enter "Google keyword tool" into Google and it's usually the top result. I highly recommend spending time researching your niche and coming up with a list of key phrases and questions that your target audience could enter into Google when looking for a solution that you provide. Plug them into the keyword tool and look at the volume of monthly searches. You will quickly identify recurring topics and themes that are "hot buttons" in your industry. You should write articles on these and post them in relevant forums as well as on your own blog. Ensure that there is a clear call to action at the end of each article, for example you could encourage readers to sign up to your blog or download a more in-depth report on the topic, or buy your products online. Don't miss this valuable opportunity to build your list or get a sale.

Social Forums

We've all been conditioned to turn to Google to answer and solve any question or puzzle that crops up in our day to day. These range from the mundane, "Why is the sky blue" - seriously, there are 246,000 searches a month on this question - to the more pressing. "How to lose weight" which generates 1.5 million searches a month. As a result, the number of specialist forums that exist on all manner of subjects has exploded. Your target market are asking questions relating to your category right now and if you are not monitoring these forums, your competitors are responding instead. As above, write a list of the key phrases that your customers might enter into Google and do just that and see what forums come up. Go and check them out, as that's where you need to hang out every now and then. When you respond to their questions and queries, create a sign-off that links back to your website or blog and if relevant, point readers to a specific article or blog you have written. Though make sure that this has a call to action at the end to drive sign-ups to your database or to turn prospects into customers.

You can use Google Alerts or Social Mentions to track and monitor keywords and phrases and alert you when they come up. To avoid being inundated with alerts, the more specific and targeted you can be, the better.

LinkedIn Answers

If you're in the business to business sector, (B2B), LinkedIn Answers is a great tool for you. You can subscribe to questions in your category and respond to the relevant one. It's a great way to demonstrate your credibility and expertise in your field. As always, don't miss the opportunity to create an ongoing connection with a prospect, encourage them to go to your website and sign up to your newsletter or webinars for regular advice on this topic.

LinkedIn Groups

Joining existing and setting up your own targeted LinkedIn groups for your niches are both great ways to build your list, as you can create and contribute to discussions and position yourself as a credible expert in your field. Running your own group has added benefits, as you can email subscribers directly and privately, whereas when you join a group all discussions are in the public domain. So, when you join other, relevant groups, connect to the members and then when you set up your own group, you can simply invite them over to yours.

OFFLINE LIST BUILDING STRATEGIES

There are also effective offline strategies for you to consider. If you have a retail presence, then you should try to capture both prospects' and customers' details at every opportunity. The fact they are in your store is usually a pre-qualifier, so think up ways to encourage prospects to give you their email and or home addresses. Here are a few ideas:

Give something away for free

Whatever you offer has to have a high perceived value for the prospect. You could run a competition to win your products or services and to be in with a chance, people need to share their contact details with you. Alternatively, offer free samples, or free consultations that require people to give you their details to sign up. Whatever your approach, make sure that you have a simple and quick mechanic to drive take up and make sure all entry forms include a tick box that allows you to contact them at a later date. If you target the B2B audience, you could ask prospects to enter their business cards into a prize draw. If you have a retail presence, floor staff can promote your competition or giveaway and encourage both browsers and customers to enter on the spot. The key is to offer something compelling and make it easy to sign up.

Target niche publications

Specialist publications exist for more niches than you or I can even think of. Go into a large newsagent and browse the magazine rack; newsagents and book stores at airports are ideal, as they have a huge selection. Identify a series of titles in your sector and contact the editors to find out what marketing opportunities they offer. Do they have a newsletter you can trial an ad in? If so, create an irresistible offer that requires people to part with their contact details, moving them from their subscriber list, into your database. Better still, could you offer to write a column for them, or an article demonstrating your expertise?

Add a link to your website at the end that takes readers to a sign up form on your website.

BUYING A LIST

It's possible to buy contact lists for more or less any niche you can think of. However, I am not a fan of bought lists as, without fail, they have been rinsed so many times that your communications fail to connect. You are also subject to the quality and accuracy of the data. Are the contacts on the list really who you think they are? Not always. If you absolutely have to buy a list and to be honest, given the above examples, I can't think of any reason why you should, then you should qualify this list using a telemarketing service first. A telemarketer can call each contact to qualify them and determine whether they are interested in your products or services. This can be expensive and time consuming and will dramatically shrink your list, but what you are left with are prospects, not strangers.

ACTION

- ☐ Make a list of non competing businesses you can approach for a joint venture, decide on the terms and conditions of your referral scheme and start calling them one by one.

- ☐ List large competitors you could approach to buy their unconverted leads.

- ☐ Write a list of all the key phrases, problems and questions that people could put into Google to find your products and services. Then use Google's keyword tool to see which are the most popular and plan out blog posts or articles for the top 5. Make sure that you review Google's related searches for additional ideas.

- ☐ Use your keyword list to search for forums to join and sign up. Add a reminder to your calendar to search the forums once a week for 30 minutes.

- ☐ Set up alerts on the key phrases so that you can respond quickly to relevant questions that position you as an expert.

- ❑ Put a reminder in your calendar to regularly review LinkedIn Answers

- ❑ Join groups relevant to your niche on LinkedIn - make sure that you look at the number of members and join the largest.

- ❑ If strategies for building offline lists are relevant to your business, decide on your mechanic - a competition, a freebie, a trial or other and agree how you will collect the data. Make sure that you ask entrants if they would be interested in receiving ongoing news, offers, emails from you.

- ❑ Research what publications exist in your niche and offer your expertise to the editors.

So, now you know how to create targeted leads, let's now explore what you do if they don't buy from you.

What do you give the person who doesn't buy from you?

> "Giving is better than receiving because
> giving starts the receiving process."
> **Jim Rohn**

Most of the companies I advise are initially pretty stumped by this question. "Nothing?" is usually the tentative reply. Nope, it's not nothing. It needs to be something that starts them on their journey with you. What this is depends on the nature of your business. It could be a free consultation, an article or case study, a link to a talk you have done or a sample of your products. In short, something that positions you as a thought leader in your field or gives them a taste of what you offer. Something that lets them try before they buy. This helps to move them from "strangers" to "prospects" and depending on how you supply this freebie, it could also mean you get their contact details at the same time and build your database. Your goal is then to convert them to a customer and move them down the funnel below.

The objective of this funnel is to move people from strangers to prospects right through to raving fans over time.

A raving fan is someone who will not only buy your latest products or services as soon as you launch them, but they will tell all their social groups just how great they are and encourage them to buy too. The ultimate customer. The theory of the funnel is that the further down they go, the more they spend with you.

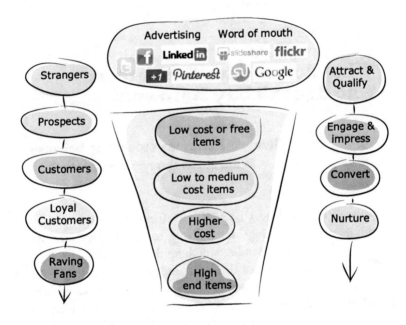

Life is not always this linear of course; a customer could buy a high end item as a first purchase and another customer might only ever buy your low to medium cost items and still be a raving fan. Flaws aside, what I do like about this model is how it challenges the way you view your product or service portfolio and the journey on which you could take your customers. It also makes you realise the importance of your products for prospects, as these are the critical starting point of your relationship.

BUILDING LOYALTY AND CREATING ADVOCATES

In today's competitive markets, packed full of undifferentiated products, service is a key differentiator and sometimes the only one. If you want to build loyalty you need to deliver an impeccable service. Finding unexpected ways to surprise and delight your customers is key. How could you make your customers feel special? What additional extras could you develop that will make them feel great about your brand? An unexpected gift on their birthday, a yearly reward for being one of your biggest customers, a "welcome to the family" pack, a mid year thank you gift? In an earlier chapter, I wrote about the importance of being disruptive in your market, over-delivering on your service is a great opportunity to do just that. Think about how you could outdo the service your competition provides. If you delight your customers, they will tell other people about it and attract more people to your brand.

CONTINUITY PROGRAMMES

Whilst it is great to get a sale, real money is made from repeat business and recurring revenue streams. Continuity programmes are different to loyalty programmes, as they involve the sale of a product or service, on a recurring basis. A local beauty salon can offer discounted massages for a monthly membership fee; they heavily discount the first one and then discount on-going. When someone signs-up to Amazon they are offered their membership programme, Amazon Prime; free one day delivery for a one off payment each year. If you know you will buy from Amazon multiple times a year, it's a no-brainer. What could you offer to generate recurring revenue? A paid "members only" area of your site with exclusive content? A similar service to Amazon? Could your customers commit to yearly or quarterly purchases and receive one every week or month? Whatever you decide, make sure it's presented in a way that makes it a no-brainer for someone to take up. It should feel like a great deal, be easily affordable and therefore an "under the radar" purchase. Continuity programmes are great for cash flow, which is critical when you are just starting out.

How to decide on a pricing strategy

"Price is what you pay. Value is what you get."
Warren Buffet

When calculating company profits there are three basic variables; cost, sales volume and price. Most businesses focus on developing cost reduction initiatives and have a level of confidence in their ability to increase sales volumes, but pricing strategies are often very simplistic. Significant resources are often put behind sophisticated technologies that monitor and control costs in great detail and in real time. Similarly, a great deal of time and effort is focused on developing sales forecasts, but the hugely important role of pricing gets comparatively little attention.

Deciding how to price your products and services can be a minefield, but it is one of the most important decisions you will make in your business. Your pricing strategy needs to be inline with your positioning and has to be driven by demand in your market.

There are some obvious considerations such as the cost to produce your product or service and your operating costs, i.e. the marketing, overheads, payroll, office supplies etc. What you add on top is where the fun begins. Too high a price and you drive your customers to your competitors, too low a price and you reduce your profit margin. If you have direct competitors then a price precedent has been set, but if they are well established and bigger, then you will most likely struggle to compete on price. So how do you determine what price is too high? Too low? Just right?

Research is critical. You need to test demand for your products and services at different prices. It's really easy to run pricing research online using Google Adwords or Facebook ads. In both instances you create a series of ads that are exactly the same bar the price. For example, if, like The Snugg you sold iPad 2 cases and wanted to identify the price at which you could sell the highest volume of your products, you would run the below ad alongside three identical ads with prices at £19.99, £25.99 and £39.99. Each would need to click through to a landing page selling the product at the advertised price and the price that delivers the highest volume sales is the winner. Interestingly, it is not always the lowest price that wins. The only way to find your pricing sweet spot is to test it.

The Snugg™ **iPad 2 Case**
www.thesnugg.com/iPad2
Best Selling Leather Case **Cover**
& Stand For **iPad** 2. Buy Now £29.99

Even if your product or service is not available online, you can still run this kind of "quick and dirty" pricing research and just measure purchase intent based on the number of people who click on your ad and the page they go to can even be a "page not found". Whilst the results are not as definitive as actual purchases, this approach still delivers useful insights. In this instance, the ad with the highest click through rate (clicks divided by impressions, an impression is when your ad is viewed once by someone online) is the most effective. That said, the truest test of a pricing strategy is when consumers vote with their wallet and you track and monitor your competitors' responses, but this at least gives you initial market feedback. Ideally you want to get about 100 clicks on each ad, so that your data is robust enough. If budgets allow, seeking the advice of a pricing strategist and running more formal pricing research is well advised. If not, read on and I'll cover some of the basic principles of pricing.

Your pricing strategy is driven by your objectives, so what do you want to achieve?

- ❑ **To drive trial?** You might consider an introductory price to gain market share.

- ❑ **To drive footfall in-store?** Your product or service could be a loss-leader designed to literally bring people through the door who will buy your other products or services that have greater profit margins. This is a strategy used by supermarkets, they often sell beer as a loss-leader as buyers invariably purchase other products once in store.

- ❑ **To maximise your profits?** This does not always mean the highest price in your market, as operating efficiencies will need to be taken into consideration.

- ❑ **To maximise unit sales?** This could mean low prices, but the focus is on getting the maximum output from your factory or through your staff.

- ❑ **To undercut the competition?** This could mean your price is lower than the leading brands, but more expensive than the other players, or you're the lowest on the market.

- ❑ **To be the most premium brand on the market?** You could position your product or service as the most exclusive on the market, commanding the highest price.

- ❑ **To block other competitors entering the market?** If profits are low, entering this market would not be very attractive, so blocking competitors can be a good way to build your customer base before you raise your prices.

PRICING STRATEGIES

Once you're clear on your objectives, it's easier to decide on your pricing strategy, so let's take a look at the different approaches to pricing.

Cost-plus pricing

This is the simplest pricing strategy and literally means that you determine your price by adding a percentage on top of all the costs associated with your goods or services. It doesn't take into consideration competitive pricing and these days it's rarely adopted.

Price skimming or creaming

High tech companies usually adopt this strategy to recoup some of the huge costs of research and development. The price is set high and they target early adopters who are the least price sensitive, as they are willing to pay high prices for the latest and greatest technological toy on the market. This strategy usually has a limited timeframe and prices then decrease to drive up market share. Every time the price is lowered, the market broadens and more units are sold. This does not necessarily mean that profits shrink, as since the launch, factories improve their capacity providing economies of scale.

This can be a risky strategy, as it only really works if you can create a monopoly for a long enough period. However, the speed competitors can develop copycat products today can mean that they enter the market soon after your launch at a lower price, whilst yours is still high.

Price discrimination

This is when you set different prices for different target audiences or situations, i.e. discounts for students and OAPs, high prices for the best seats in the house, lower prices for matinées versus evening performances.

Penetration pricing

You set a low introductory price to attract customers and drive up market share. Prices are often increased once market share is achieved. However, raising the price is not always easy. It helps if you can increase production efficiencies as demand increases to ensure you get an acceptable profit margin.

Premium pricing

A high price creates a perception of high quality, as many people believe the price of a product reflects the quality. This is not, of course, always justified, but the perception can be reinforced by packaging, advertising and where the product is stocked. Interestingly, when it comes to the premium end of the market, the usual market principles do not apply, as lower prices do not increase demand; often the higher the price, the higher the demand.

Tied product pricing

This is when the entry product has a low price and is often sold at a loss, while associated products or services are aggressively priced. Razor blade companies use this model; the razor is sold at a low price, whilst the replacement blades are where they make a profit. Mobile phones are another example, the phones are free, and they make a profit on voice and text packages. Printers and refill cartridges are another example.

The challenge with this strategy is that the associated products can be copied and sold more cheaply by competitors. An example of this is the rather aggressive price under-cutting by generic ink cartridge suppliers. To fight back some printer makers claim warranties can be invalidated through use of competitor ink-cartridges. The price war is an on-going challenge for this sector.

Dynamic pricing

This is when prices are changed according to demand. This strategy is used a lot by airlines and hotels, as demand increases, prices rise. Advances in IT have enabled some e-commerce sites take this approach a step further, they tailor the price of goods to the user based on their purchase history and their willingness to pay a certain price. Supermarkets use dynamic pricing strategies for their price promises; they lower their prices based on competitors' prices for the same goods.

So, as you can see, there's a lot to consider when thinking about how to price your goods and services. The wrong pricing strategy can kill your business before it even gets started. The "right price" is all about the perception of value that you create. If a potential customer tells you that your prices are too high, this means you haven't created enough value and you need to address this. One last point to remember is that it is always easier to lower your prices than to raise them.

ACTION

☐ Run an online test to research the right price for your products or services, even if they are already on the market. Find out how much of a price premium your market can accept.

☐ Have you anticipated your competitors' reactions to your pricing strategy? Could your approach create a price war, if so, how will you react?

☐ Do you know whether your consumers are willing to pay a price premium for additional features and benefits? You can explore this through online ad research, use the copy to describe the additional features and play around with the prices. Make sure that you only change one element of each ad at a time, otherwise you will not know what is driving the change in the volume of clicks.

☐ Think about your long term pricing strategy; do you intend to increase your prices each year? By how much? In line with inflation? Lower? Look at pricing trends in your market, do your suppliers increase their prices yearly? What do your competitors do?

UNDERSTANDING
BUYING BEHAVIOUR

The only three types of sales

"A budget tells us what we can't afford, but it doesn't keep us from buying it."

William Feather

There are only ever three types of sales:

1. Buying something for the first time.
2. Repeat purchase of something you have bought before.
3. Switching to a new model or brand in the same category.

The hardest sale to make is trying to persuade someone to buy something for the first time, as most people hesitate. This hesitation is driven by a mix of emotions; fear of loss, curiosity and a desire for gain. It's therefore vital that your communications focus on minimising the risk of purchase and amplifying the gain.

Repeat purchase products are the easiest sale and can be fairly predictable if you understand the average consumption times for your products, or the average frequency that someone takes up your services. However, nothing can be left to chance and timely communications should keep your brand on their purchasing list. If you sell ink cartridges and you identify that, on average, a particular segment of your consumers buy new cartridges every month, then on the twenty-fifth day send them an email reminding them how easy it is to buy online and how frustrating it is to run out of ink. Similarly if you sell a seasonal product such as sun tan lotion, or swimwear, a pre summer holiday communication is effective and timely.

Getting consumers to change their behaviour and switch brands can be a challenging sale, although it can be relatively easy if your competitors have upset their consumers in some way, but you can't wait around for that to happen. There are various factors that impact on the willingness of someone to switch brands:

- ❑ How easy it is to switch.

- ❑ The length of time someone has repeatedly bought a particular product or service - if a habit has not been established, it is easier to encourage a switch.

- ❑ If consumers believe that they will get a better product or service elsewhere.

- ❑ If an issue is unsatisfactorily resolved by a competitor.

When trying to drive switching behaviour, communications should focus on what makes your product or service unique and if it's desired by consumers then you stand a greater chance of driving switching behaviour. However, even though your brand might be demonstrably better, it does not mean that consumers will jump ship as soon as they hear this. Most people are creatures of habit; just consider how poor the service we receive from banks can be and despite this, the number of people who actually switch is still relatively small. If your industry is full of "me too" products or services and you're not sure what makes you unique in your market, it helps to understand why people buy the products and services in your sector, so let's delve into this.

Why people buy

"The basic difference between emotion
and reason is that emotion leads to action,
whilst reason leads to conclusions"
Donald Caine

It's important to understand why people buy your products and services, so that you can tailor your communications and connect with your audience in a relevant and compelling way. There are different generic models that claim to define a consumer's decision making process. They go a little something like this:

Seems pretty straightforward, right? Let's run through an example. It starts with the realisation that something is not as it should be, so a car struggles to start every morning and has difficulty accelerating. The owner then considers various ways to solve the problem - this is the second step. He or she could buy a new car, a second hand car, get the car repaired, take the bus, a taxi, or even rollerblade to work. The third step is the evaluation of these alternatives. Rollerblades are inexpensive, but not that practical on cold and rainy days, the budget might not stretch to a new car etc. Then he or she decides what to buy and might end up returning the car if it doesn't live up to expectations.

Now whilst this outlines a very logical and linear approach to decision making, in reality, the process is rarely this linear, as someone might go back and forth evaluating alternatives and researching more or less before purchase. Furthermore, the speed with which they move through this process will also vary dramatically depending on the type of product that they're buying. Products that are expensive, e.g. cars, houses, or of great importance, such as acne medication will have a more considered approach compared with a bottle of water bought on impulse while out shopping on a hot day. The biggest issue, is that it doesn't consider the huge role that emotions play in the decision making process. As Freud pointed out, "we are motivated by conscious and unconscious forces", yet this is not reflected in this incredibly rational model. To really understand what drives purchase in your category you need to understand the emotional triggers and critically what can influence these triggers. I strongly believe that your brand and communications need to create an emotional response, as this is the highest form of interaction, but to truly be able to connect emotionally with your target it helps to first look at the fundamental human emotions.

Robert Plutchik, psychologist and leading expert on the research of emotions, believed that there are eight basic, primary emotions, each with a polar opposite and that all other emotions are a combination of these. Like colours, each emotion can exist in varying degrees of intensity or levels of arousal.

Basic Emotion	Polar Opposite
Joy	Sadness
Trust	Disgust
Fear	Anger
Surprise	Anticipation

When it comes to your brand and your communications, what type of emotional response do you want to create? The success of some anti-smoking campaigns is down to their ability to create disgust through provocative images highlighting the damage that every cigarette causes to internal organs. To drive up donations, charities often make people feel sad by showing images of deprived and suffering children, or forlorn, abandoned dogs. Cadbury's famous "gorilla" TV ad intended to make viewers feel pure joy through utter absurdity; a gorilla playing the drums to a Phil Collins' track, it certainly touched the nation. Emotional communications are significantly more effective than rational, but don't just take my word for it. In the brilliant book, "Marketing in the Era of Accountability" by Les Binet and Peter Fields, the authors prove this point in spades. Using evidence from 880 case studies from the IPA Databank (Institute of Practitioners in Advertising), they demonstrate that emotionally based campaigns are not only likely to produce very large business effects but also produce more of them, outperforming rational campaigns on every single business measure.

To watch the anti smoking and Cadbury's gorilla ad, go to www.jacquelinebiggs.com/ads

INTERNAL AND EXTERNAL INFLUENCES

There are a number of other factors that also influence purchasing decisions. These can be classified as "internal", how we think and feel and "external", how our surroundings make us think and feel. It is useful to create a written profile of your target audience considering each of these influences.

INTERNAL: PSYCHOGRAPHICS

Psychographics explore how a consumer's personality, values, attitudes, interests and lifestyle influence their purchasing decisions. Some people are "bargain hunters" and won't stop until they are sure they have the best price for a product or service. Others just like variety, and some people are simply more receptive to the excitement of trying something new. Political opinions, attitudes to the environment and sport allegiances can also impact purchasing decisions. Just look at the growth in demand for organic foods or products perceived to be environmentally friendly.

Attitudes and behaviour change as people move through different stages of life. A family with young children is likely to have a very different lifestyle to empty nesters; couples whose children have left home. As a result, there are significant differences in buying patterns between the two groups. There are four main stages in a typical lifestyle and each can be further divided according to income and occupation. Which life stage are your products or services targeting? If more than one. how do you adapt their positioning to increase the relevance to each audience?

Motivation

Unlocking the motivation for purchase is where it gets really interesting, but it's not always easy. What people say and what they really mean are not always the same. A teenage boy heading out on a date might buy a deodorant to prevent stinky armpits that night, but really he wants to make sure that nothing will stop him from getting laid that evening. Understanding this motivation takes the brand down a very different communication route. This was the killer insight behind Lynx' "spray more, get more" campaign, you can read the case study at the end of this chapter. Some people might be unwilling to admit the real motivation behind a purchase, because it's embarrassing, or it shows them in a bad light. For others it might be latent and unknown even to them. There is no substitute for talking to your target audience, so if you're not sure what the core motivation for purchase is in your sector, then you need to find a way to gain an insight. In the next chapter I outline research techniques that will help you to get the insights you need.

Involvement

The level of interest in a product or service, coupled with the importance of it to the buyer, influences decisions. Buying a new car is vastly different to buying a smoothie, the first is a very involved and important purchase and the second far less so. As involvement increases, consumers are more motivated to find out more about a product or service before purchase. That said, a new trend is emerging due to the explosion of social media and the speed with which people can connect with corporations, more and more consumers are demanding a greater level of transparency than ever before for both low interest and high interest categories. I explore this in greater depth in the chapter, "Why the consumer - and not you - is in charge". What comes up when your brand gets "Googled"? Make sure consumers see what you want them to see.

Degree of loyalty

Loyalty positively impacts upon buying decisions. Consumers who buy one brand, either all, or most of the time, are a company's most valuable consumers. Spending time identifying your loyalists and creating marketing that specifically focuses on retaining these customers, can be more profitable than trying to recruit new customers, as the cost of acquisition has already been accounted for. However, no matter which category you are in, today's loyal consumers might not be tomorrow's; if you keep this thought at the forefront of your mind and find meaningful ways to surprise and delight your customers on-going, you will retain them for longer.

EXTERNAL: COLLECTIVE INFLUENCES

The second type of influence on buying behaviour is from our surrounding environment and is referred to as collective influences.

Culture

Cultural factors can have a significant impact on buying behaviour, as they can be the most basic cause of a person's wants and behaviour. Growing up, children learn basic values, perception and wants from their family, friends and peers and this influences what they find desirable. Nationality also impacts what and why people buy; for example, Indian and Polish people have very distinct food tastes and this is reflected in their shopping basket. Popular culture is also a big influence, just consider the impact Mad Men has had on fashion; it spawned a capsule collection at Banana Republic and influenced Prada's Spring 2012 runway collection. It's important to try and spot "cultural shifts" and trends as they happen, as these can identify new product opportunities, as well as increase demand for existing products and services.

Social class

There are six official social classes in the UK, as outlined in the following chart, and these are widely used to profile and predict different customer behaviour. The classifications are determined by a combination of income, occupation, education, wealth and other variables. Social class determines to some extent, the type, quality and quantity of products or services that a person buys or uses. In the UK the supermarket from which you choose to buy your food often reflects your class; discount chains, Aldi and Lidl have more lower class shoppers, whilst Waitrose, renowned for its superior quality food, has a higher percentage of affluent shoppers. However, the classifications are not entirely accurate when you consider that plumbers and electricians would be classified as C2 - skilled workers, one of the lower social ranks, but in actual fact their level of income could be the same as class B, the Middle class, or maybe even higher. Consumer behaviour cannot be determined by social class alone, but the members of each class do share similar buying behaviour.

Class Name	Social Status	Occupational Head of Household	% of UK Population
A	Upper Middle	These are professional people, very senior managers in business or commerce or top-level civil servants. Retired people, previously grade A, and their widows.	3
B	Middle	Middle management executives in large organisations, with appropriate qualifications. Principal officers in local government and civil service. Top management or owners of small business concerns, educational and service establishments. Retired people, previously grade B, and their widows.	20
C1	Lower Middle	Junior management, owners of small establishments, and all others in non-manual positions. Jobs in this group have very varied responsibilities and educational requirements. Retired people, previously grade C1, and their widows.	28
C2	Skilled Working	All skilled manual workers, and those manual workers with responsibility for other people. Retired people, previously grade C2, with pensions from their job. Widows, if receiving pensions from their late husband's job.	21
D	Working	All semi-skilled and un-skilled manual workers, apprentices and trainees to skilled workers. Retired people, previously grade D, with pensions from their job. Widows, if receiving a pension from their late husband's job.	18
E	Lowest level of subsistence	All those entirely dependent on the state long-term, through sickness, unemployment, old age or other reasons. Those unemployed for a period exceeding six months (otherwise classify on previous occupation). Casual workers and those without a regular income. Only households without a Chief Income Earner will be coded in this group.	10

5

5   Source: Occupation Groupings: A Job Dictionary, 6ed, 2006, The Market Research Society

Reference Groups

Friends, colleagues and acquaintances can exert a huge influence over big and small buying decisions. With increasing distrust in advertising and the Media, word of mouth and recommendations from friends and family have never been more powerful. Similarly, famous endorsements can also sway buying behaviour, which is why Justin Bieber and Brand Beckham are forever in demand. Reference groups can be separated into three types: aspirational, associative and dissociative. Understanding which has the greatest influence can lead to very effective communications.

- ❏ The aspirational reference group represents someone you would like to be; film stars, athletes, pop stars etc.

- ❏ The associative reference group represents the people who are more or less the same as you; family, friends, colleagues etc.

- ❏ The dissociative reference group represents people you don't want to be like; a teenage mum, the homeless, the overweight etc. The literally named store, The Gap, came about because many younger people wanted to actively dissociate from parents and other older and "uncool" people.

EXTERNAL: ENVIRONMENTAL INFLUENCES

Time of day, time of year, weather and temperature all influence buying decisions. Beer sales are highest in summer and spike over very hot weekends, DIY products spike over bank holiday weekends, car sales slow at Christmas and products for people suffering from seasonal affective disorder start to ramp up in September. To avoid seasonal dips, companies often try to extend the occasions for their products. Kellogg's promotes its Special K cereal as suitable for any meal time, rather than just for breakfast, for example. It's important to understand the trends in your market and prepare for them.

The occasion for which a product or service is purchased or consumed is also a key driver of behaviour. If your product is bought as a gift, this requires a very different style of communication to when it is bought for personal use. Many companies develop products to specifically target different occasions. Ferrero Rocher created smaller, four chocolate packs, for individual consumption to be sold alongside their large gift boxes. Bottled water companies target multiple occasions with sports caps for the gym, two-litre bottles for sharing and smaller bottles for on-the-go consumption. Can you bundle or un-bundle your products or services to appeal to different occasions? Understanding the occasions on which your consumers buy your products and services is key to shaping your communications. Furthermore, finding and promoting new occasions for your brand can be an effective way to grow your customer base.

SUMMARY

A person's buying behaviour is the result of the complex interplay of all these cultural, social, personal, and psychological factors. You can't control these factors, but they are useful in identifying and understanding the consumers you are trying to influence through your communications.

Case Study: Unilever - Lynx deodorant

The deodorant market was categorised by functional benefits for years, it followed a classic problem-solution model. The problem was stinky armpits, the solution was fragrance. That was until Unilever's Lynx entered the market.

The Lynx brand team knew their target audience, 17-19 year-old boys, intimately. They knew that they were obsessed with how to get a girl and decided to associate themselves with the one thing their target audience spent so much time thinking about. So the "Lynx Effect" campaign was born. Lynx was positioned as the brand that hot girls just couldn't get enough of and the ads showed women being overwhelmed with desire to get up close and personal with Lynx-wearing men. This was an entirely different way of looking at the category's benefits. Yes, the avoidance of stinky pits was important, but there was

---

a far more motivating benefit for them that no deodorant brand was communicating. Smelly armpits are a huge turn off for the ladies. Flip that around and become the brand that helps you to pull women and you're engaging your hot-blooded male audience. Of course it's hyperbole, but it worked and sales went through the roof. That was back in 1999, and then in 2005 they launched a raunchy new campaign with the self styled "purveyor of pulling". With an objective to get their target to use even more Lynx, these tongue in cheek ads looked at what might happen if men spray Lynx in unexpected places. In one spot, the star of the ad sprays Lynx liberally on mud. Consequently, two young women on horses nearby are compelled to rip off their clothes in excitement and cover each other in mud. They then beckon the Lynx-sprayer to join them with the end-line:

"Spray more, get more."

A similar phenomenon occurs when Lynx is sprayed on kitchen surfaces. On entering the room, a woman drops her shopping to rub herself along the trail of Lynx spray… The most lauded ad shows thousands of bikini clad babes racing through the woods desperate to reach the Lynx guy spraying himself liberally with the deodorant all over this body and ends with the same tagline: "Spray more get more. The Lynx effect." In 2011, the campaign evolved, but the "Lynx" effect continued with an ad showing how even angels will fall for a man wearing Lynx. To watch these campaigns go to: www.jacquelinebiggs.com/Lynx

Not only is it a great campaign, encouraging liberal application of the deodorant also meant that guys needed to buy it more frequently, which is clearly good for business. Generating more than £100 million a year in retail sales in the men's toiletries market, it clearly pays to challenge your market and connect with your consumers on a deeper level.

ACTION

☐ What is the one emotion that you want your brand to evoke? Look back at your existing communications, including your website and consider how effectively this is being communicated. Change the copy if it is not.

☐ Create a profile for each of your target audiences based on the internal and external influences. Make it visual, add photos of your ideal consumer and pictures of what influences him or her. The more vividly and accurately you describe your target, the easier it is to create communication that connects with their needs, wants and motivations. If you are struggling to build an accurate profile then plug gaps in your knowledge with actual research with your target audience. Don't just guess. Read "How to research buying behaviour" for ideas on how to gain insights into your target.

☐ What occasions do your products and services target? Can you reach more by bundling or unbundling your products or services?

How to research buying behaviour

"Research is creating new knowledge."
Neil Armstrong

Whilst there are different models that help to explain buying behaviour, the only way to truly get under the skin of what drives purchase in your market is to observe and ask your consumers. This sounds pretty obvious I know, but it's surprising how few companies do this.

QUANT VS QUAL

Research is divided into two categories; qualitative (qual) and quantitative (quant). Qual research is the more "touchy feely" side of research, it explores how people think and feel and can be incredibly insightful. It's a great complement to a larger quant study, as it allows you to get behind the numbers and unlock some powerful insights. For this reason it's often used as a precursor to a larger quant study, as it's a great way to identify issues or trends that can be explored by a more statistically robust quant study. It's conducted amongst a smaller sample size than quant surveys, so it is not statistically viable and requires a trained moderator to get the most out of this type of research. Although, if budgets can't extend to payment of a moderator, you should still do this yourself, rather than run no consumer research at all.

Quant research is all about the numbers and usually requires people to fill out a survey. Before the emergence of companies like Survey Monkey and Survey Gizmo, you had to approach a research agency to run the study for you, but today it is really easy to create professional looking surveys quickly and cheaply.

When it comes to deciding which type of research will be the most effective, it really depends on the nature of your business. For example, if your company sells a solution for thrush, approaching someone in-store and asking them why they buy your product would be pretty inappropriate, but emailing an online survey to your target audience will get a much higher response. Weigh up the pros and cons of each of the following.

GETTING FAST INSIGHTS

If your products are stocked in a retail outlet, go and watch your consumers at what's referred to as "the moment of truth", the moment in-store when they make their brand selection, aside from your time, it's free and can be a great source of insight. Whilst you're there, ask the retail assistants the types of questions they get asked, as they're at the coal face and involved in helping consumers choose between brands and products.

If you're an online retailer, create a short survey that consumers fill out post purchase. Identify who they are and explore the reasons behind their purchase, who they're buying for and why. Keep it short and snappy and offer an incentive for completing the survey such as discounts on future purchases. The disadvantage to running a survey is that it relies on reported behaviour, which is not as powerful as observation, but it can help you to profile your consumers and get some fast answers.

Depending on what you need to know you could also create a poll on your site, it is quick to complete and a great way to get a quick response about anything from a new product idea to packaging designs. Both Survey Monkey and Survey Gizmo offer online polls.

If you are looking for more robust market information then Mintel and Datamonitor offer comprehensive market intelligence reports that look at how big a market is in both volume and value terms, whether it is in growth or decline and how it is segmented; they also pull apart the key players by looking at their share of the market and exploring the key drivers of purchase. What they won't tell you of course, is why people buy or don't buy your particular brand, but they do give you solid insights into your market. To find out if reports exist for your category you can search online at the following locations:

- www.datamonitor.com
- http://store.mintel.com

Focus groups are fairly formal chats with around six to eight members of your target audience and a moderator leading the conversation. It's important to run three or four groups to ensure learnings are consistent. They are a great way to get a response to an issue, quickly identify any problems with creative ideas, or to get a feedback to products or concepts. However, when it comes to identifying why people buy, they can have limitations as the responses are all claimed behaviour rather than actual and a group effect can come into play, meaning someone might not want to voice their opinion if it contradicts the rest.

> When I was the strategy planner on Foster's lager, we used to regularly run "accompanied drinking sessions". These involved getting about eight 18-24 year-old blokes together in a few local pubs; we usually recruited friendship pairs so they were more relaxed. We bought them beers all night, Foster's of course and chatted to them about various topics. It was always incredibly insightful and a great way for some of the senior members of the client team to meet their target audience, as they were often more than twice their age.

As mentioned earlier, if budgets don't allow you to hire trained researchers, it's better to run the research yourself, than have none at all, although make sure that you don't reveal that it's your company, as this can skew the responses. I also recommend against recruiting people within your company to come along, as employees will have a different view on your company, brand and products than target consumers outside the office. Instead, if you have people who represent your target audience working for you, ask them to recruit their friends, but make sure that they don't reveal which company the research is for. Depending on the subject of the research, you probably want to run it away from the office to avoid disclosing your brand. If budget allows, do hire a moderator as to get the best results the discussion needs to be impartial, without any leading questions. If you need help to recruit the right people then Google "focus group recruitment" for companies offering this service.

Depth interviews are similar to focus groups, but involve only one or two people being interviewed at one time and as the name indicates, they are much more in depth. There is no set duration, as it depends entirely on what you need to cover, but rarely go beyond two hours. They are ideal for investigating sensitive, personal or confidential information that respondents might be reluctant to talk about in a group environment. They're also great for researching people with busy lifestyles who would struggle to attend a focus group; doctors, senior business people, solo parents etc, as they can take place in their home, in the workplace, or even on the phone. As before, you can contact companies to help you with recruitment, or to moderate if you need it.

ACTION

❑ Do you really know why your consumers buy your products or services? If not, list what you need to know and decide on your budget and which research technique to use.

❑ Even when you think you know the key motivations of purchase, it is still sensible to sense check these through research. Just because you have always believed something, doesn't make it right.

❑ Once you have the results of your research, review your communications. Do they address the identified needs and wants of your target audience? If not, change the copy.

The six reasons your customers leave you

> "Indifference and neglect often do much
> more damage than outright dislike."
> **J.K. Rowling**

The average business spends six times more money recruiting new customers than it does retaining existing. This is actually madness when you consider that a loyal customer can be worth more than ten times the price of a single purchase. What's even worse is that most companies have no idea why their customers leave, as typically a business hears from only 4%[6] of its dissatisfied customers. The other 96% quietly disappear and 91% will never come back. That is a serious financial hit. On the other hand, it's a massive opportunity for companies that know how to treat their customers.

According to Michael LeBoeuf's[7] extensive research with companies large and small, there are six reasons that your customers leave you.

Perceived indifference and unresolved conflicts represent 82% of the reasons - this is huge. This means that you, or your company as a whole, are to blame for your customers leaving you. Perceived indifference usually stems from customers thinking that you don't care about them or the business they give you.

6   How To Win Customers & Keep Them For Life By Michael LeBoeuf
7   How To Win Customers & Keep Them For Life By Michael LeBoeuf

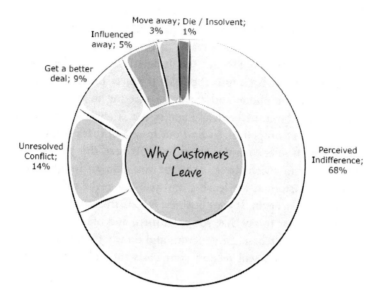

Move away; Die / Insolvent;
3% 1%

Influenced
away; 5%

Get a better
deal; 9%

Unresolved
Conflict;
14%

Why Customers
Leave

Perceived
Indifference;
68%

A lack of regular communication is usually to blame. Your customers want to hear from you and you are missing a trick if you don't create regular, follow up communications. It could be a simple email series that starts with an after sales email checking to see if they're happy with their purchase. Follow this up with some news about what you're up to in the world, then later suggest a relevant product or service they might like to try, or tell them about a relevant discount or promotion you have on. And so it continues, a mix of news and timely promotions. These emails can all be automated, the trigger to start is when they purchase your product or service. Simple, but very effective. It's also mutually beneficial, they want to hear from you and you want them to buy from you again. If you work in the business to business sector, this approach also works well and you can add in follow up phone calls and meetings into the mix for the added personal touch.

When it comes to unresolved conflict you have to get to the bottom of it and it helps to be ready to eat humble pie. You have no idea what happened, it could have been due to an altercation with one of your sales team, or because they received an unsatisfactory response to an issue. It doesn't matter. What does, is bringing them back into the fold. If you're in the B2B sector, pick up the phone and arrange a meeting to discuss their business and be empathetic and apologetic. They have probably switched to a competitor, so find out how well that's going and give them an offer to entice them back. At best, this works and they decide to switch back, at worst you gain an insight into why your customers are leaving and you can make sure that it doesn't happen again. If your business is B2C then send an email or write a letter to say that you miss them and offer a discount on their next purchase. Be generous and do what it takes to win them back as you will recoup your costs through repeat purchases in the long term.

STRATEGIES TO REVERSE DEFECTION

Give something away for free. If the average customer spend is £40, offer them a voucher for £30, chances are they will spend more than £40 thanks to the free money, but what's more important is that you are recreating the habit that they spend with you.

I advised a nutritionist client to offer a free consultation to her lapsed clients, the majority of them took it up and over 50% turned into paying clients again.

A landscape gardener client offered a free lawn mowing service to his largest lapsed clients. It got him back on their radar and gave him the perfect opportunity to suggest additional jobs.

Send gifts in the post that will surprise and delight your former customers - the main focus is to remind them that you exist, as chances are they have forgotten about you as time has gone by.

If you devise a strategy to solely address these two issues, the rewards could be fantastic, particularly as Le Boeuf also reveals that 70% of customers would do business with you again if you resolve the complaint in their favour. What's more, if you resolve it on the spot, 95% will do business with you again. This is a phenomenal insight for any business owner.

So how do you identify lapsed customers? Every business has them. Consider the average buying cycle of a customer; if it's monthly and they haven't bought from your for three months, they're a lapsed customer. If it's quarterly and they haven't bought from you for six months, they're a lapsed customer. Create a list and contact them all, you will be amazed at what this simple strategy can do to your bottom line.

ACTION

- ☐ Identify your lapsed customers and prioritise the list based on highest spenders as you will target these first.
- ☐ Plan your strategy to bring them back into the fold.
- ☐ To lower your rate of attrition set up regular communications with new and existing clients.
- ☐ Track and evaluate the impact that regular communication has on the number of lapsed customers each month. I expect it to decrease versus previous months.

Why the consumer - and not you - is in charge

> "Forget words like 'hard sell' and 'soft sell'.
> That will only confuse you. Just be sure
> your advertising is saying something with
> substance, something that will inform and
> serve the consumer, and be sure you're
> saying it like it's never been said before."
> **William Bernbach**

I've touched on the path that people follow pre purchase; problem identification, search for information, evaluation of alternatives and then potential purchase, but there is something else, about which you need to be acutely aware when planning your communications. In early 2011, Google released the results of a shopper behaviour research study commissioned through Shopper Sciences and conducted amongst 5,000 shoppers over twelve categories. The study is called ZMOT (Zero Moment Of Truth) and is well worth a read. The research explores the sources that influence shoppers' buying decisions and reveals the new decision making moment that advances in technology have created. That is the moment when we all take to our laptops or smart phones and go to Google to get more information about a topic, issue, product or service that we have just been talking about or want to know more about. Decisions are made using ratings, reviews, asking friends on social media, watching videos and reading articles. Now "pre-shopping" is of course not new, we've all researched purchases both on and offline, but primarily for big ticket items. What's changed is that "pre-shopping" now applies to all categories of shopping, large and small.

Traditionally marketers have devoted a lot of time to what Proctor & Gamble refer to as the first and second moments of truth:

> "The best brands consistently win two moments of truth. The first moment occurs at the store shelf, when a consumer decides whether to buy one brand or another. The second occurs at home, when she uses the brand -- and is delighted, or isn't."
>
> **A.G. Lafley, Proctor & Gamble CEO**[8]

Now Google is saying that whilst they continue to be important, decisions are also made before they even get in store, at the zero moment of truth online.

The most important learning from this study is that in 2010, the average shopper used 5.3 sources of information to make a decision. In 2011, this number has nearly doubled to 10.4! That's a gigantic leap. The sources range from articles, videos, product comparisons, recommendations from friends and family to ratings, testimonials, comments on blogs and websites.

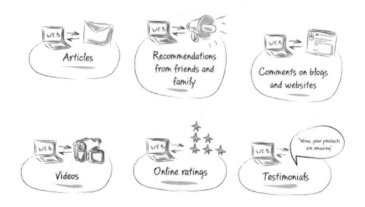

84% of shoppers said that this information shapes their decision, shifting them from undecided to decided. So the big question for you, is what happens when your brand or product gets

8 Source: Foreword to Lovemarks by Kevin Roberts

"Googled"? How many sources of information are there on your products and services? Do you have a blog, online articles, social media accounts, online product reviews and or ratings? How many? If less than 11, you need to address this right now. If you have a local business, it's still important to be found online, 20% of Google's searches are local, this then doubles to 40% for mobile searches. If you're not visible online, your consumers are going to your competitors who are.

Don't underestimate the power of reviews and ratings. A lot of companies fear low ratings, so are reluctant to give consumers the option to rate their products on their site. This is a mistake. Negative comments add authenticity, it's not possible to please everyone, that's life. Your ratings should reflect this. Of course it can be disheartening to have a negative review, but take a look at any rating sites and you'll see that the positive reviews far outweigh the negative. What's more, in some cases consumers who love your products respond to your detractors on your behalf. You can't stop the conversations about your brand, they're happening whether you like it or not, but it's much better to know what's being said and to be a part.

ACTION

❑ Enter the name of your product or service into Google and see what comes up.

❑ Next enter the name and add the word "reviews".

❑ Now do a search using "best" and your category, e.g. Best dentist in London, Best printer in Bristol. This is what your customers see when they make buying decisions in your category. Do you show up?

❑ Plan 3 ways to increase your visibility online - consider the following:

- Get featured on independent review sites.
- Contact influential bloggers in your category and ask them to review your products.
- Write articles that position you as a thought leader.

- Create blog posts on highly searched terms in your sector.
- Create short "how to" videos for your products.
- Create product demo videos.
- Create video case studies.
- Encourage video testimonials from customers and clients.
- Get social - sign up to Twitter, Facebook pages, Google+, Pinterest, YouTube, as these rate highly on Google search results.

STOP ADVERTISING AND START ENGAGING

How to create a content marketing strategy

"It is not the strongest of the species that survives, nor the most intelligent, but the one most responsive to change"
Darwin

THE THREE TYPES OF CONTENT

For years, the advertising industry has talked about the three types of content; POEM: Paid, Owned and Earned Media. In today's social world, this delineation has become obsolete. It serves only to distinguish between the differing roles media, PR and advertising agencies had in the past. Today thinking of paid and earned as separate entities will get you into strategic hot water. Every single piece of content you create needs to focus on becoming "earned".

Paid

This is advertising you pay for and for which you control the creation and distribution - print, radio, PPC, digital ads.

Owned

These are the branded assets that your company pays for to promote your brand - packaging, vehicles, retail presence.

Earned

This refers to what people say about your brand, as well as the ratings, reviews and shares you receive across social media. It's brand related content that is user generated.

YOU NEED A CONTENT MARKETING STRATEGY

Content marketing is when you create, publish and promote informational content, so blog posts, articles, white papers, case studies and videos. When you create the content online, you can tag it with keywords so that it can be found through search engines and shared by your target audience. There is a three step process to a content marketing strategy:

1. Research the questions your target audience are asking about your category.

2. Create content that answers their questions, positions your company as an authority and your products and services as a solution.

3. Promote the content so that it can be easily found.

An effective content marketing strategy is a great way to drive qualified traffic to your site, build your list, generate leads and ultimately make more sales. Content marketing is, by definition, targeted, so wastage is minimal and quality eyeballs are high. It's ideal for entrepreneurs on limited budgets.

SO HOW DO YOU FIND OUT WHAT PEOPLE WANT?

You need to put yourself in the shoes of your target market and identify the keywords that they enter into Google that relate to your products and services. In an earlier chapter, I suggested you create a list of these questions or phrases, review the list and make sure it includes phrases that relate to bigger issues or interests your niche might have where you can demonstrate your credibility. For example, if you are a decorator, you could create content on the seven mistakes to avoid when putting up wall-paper, the exact phrase "how to hang wallpaper" is searched for 1,600 times a month. If you sell kitchen utensils, you could recommend the best knife set to buy and demonstrate how to use it, there are almost 2,000 monthly searches for the exact phrase "chefs knives". You get the idea. Next enter your keywords into Google's keyword tool and review how many monthly searches there are on each term. Google also suggests related keywords, which is where it gets really interesting, as without fail this generates surprising results. The longer and more specific your phrase, the more targeted and relevant your content will be. To find additional keywords, you can also enter competitors' web addresses and Google scrapes their site and lists their keywords. When selecting your keywords you need to ensure that there are enough monthly searches each month to warrant creating content on your keywords.

> TIP: Market Samurai is a paid keyword tool that provides a more sophisticated level of keyword research, so it's worth looking into if budgets allow.

Once you know what your target audience are looking for, you can create the appropriate content; the more that you can create for each keyword phrase the better. How you tag and title your content is critical to un-targeting those it's not designed for. Most people don't think in this way, but it's important. Don't waste people's time, make it really clear in the subject header of your email, the header of your article and the title of your video what they will get. Being ambiguous will give you false reads on the success of your content, so tighten your titles.

CONTENT MARKETING STRATEGY TIPS

When you first start out, planning a content strategy can be daunting. How on earth will you find the time to do all of this and run a company? In part it's about finding a routine that works for you, but following are a few tips. Once you are clear on your strategy, you can always outsource the development of the content if you need to.

1. Establish a frequency

You might not need, or want, to blog, tweet and update your status daily, but monthly is not often enough. Create a schedule that works for you and stick to it, as once you stop, it can be hard to re-start. Map-out possible white papers, blog post ideas, interviews, video content in advance and create a content calendar for the next few months.

2. Regular items

What could you do regularly that's valuable to your audience and low maintenance? A view on the week that was, an insider's tip, a book review? Consider creating themes for days of the week, last Friday of the month could be a case study day, the first Monday of the month could be a video day and so on. This sets an expectation and is a good way to stay top of mind, as your readers or viewers will start to look out for it if they enjoy your content.

3. Leverage technology

When you come across something great on the web that you want to share, make sure that you capture it and save it for easy posting or reference later. I use three online tools for this, so Google them and see what works for you:

- ❏ **Evernote:** Great for multimedia note-taking, archiving and easy search.
- ❏ **Delicious:** Bookmark and file things for later.
- ❏ **BufferApp:** Instantly tweet or post content you find online, or set a time for a later post.

4. Guest posts or interviews

Who would your audience be interested in hearing from? You could interview them or ask them to write a guest blog post and make it a regular feature if it is well received.

5. Turn on feedback options

No matter where your content sits, make sure that you turn on comments and feedback options such as ratings, votes etc. It's a great way to see how well you're doing and to identify the type of content that excites your audience. This will give you lots of ideas for future content.

6. Listen and participate

It goes without saying that you need to participate in conversations on your own channels with engaged readers and listeners, but don't forget to listen into conversations happening in your industry, what are other people saying? It's the social media equivalent to getting out of the house. Comment on other people's blogs and in forums and link back to your content. Use Google Alerts to keep up with what's being said online in your industry and once you identify the key blogs in your sector consider setting up Google Reader so you have all your RSS feeds in one place for speedy review.

7. Promote, promote, promote

Creating great content takes time and it would be criminal if no one could find it. To be effective your content needs to be promoted and distributed properly to gain traction. As soon as you create a blog post or a new video promote it across every platform. Tweet about it, update your status on Facebook, Google+ and LinkedIn, blog about it, Pin it, email your subscribers, comment in relevant forums or on related blog posts and link back to your content. You can also upload presentations, videos and webinars onto Slideshare which further increases their reach. Next think about where you could potentially syndicate your content, who are the influencers in your market that you could create specific guest posts for or share content on? See the chapter, "How to send your blog viral" for tips on how to find high traffic blogs.

8. Include a call to action

At the end of every piece of content you need to have a clear call to action. What is the one thing that you want people to do when they get to the end of your case study, video, article, blog post? Is it to share it, to comment, to contact you for more information, to buy something? Be very clear and be very single-minded, but do not waste this opportunity with engaged readers and viewers.

Getting to grips with Google's keyword tool

1. Go to https://adwords.google.com/select/KeywordToolExternal
2. Sign in with a Google account.
3. Enter your list of keywords - one on each line.
4. Check "Exact" on the left hand side - this gives you the actual volume of searches for that specific term, as opposed to that term in a longer sentence (phrase and broad)
5. Google will suggest related keywords underneath those you entered.
6. Look for low competition and high search volume, as the higher the competition, the harder it is to rank for your selected word. If your niche is highly competitive then you will need to search for less competitive keywords, which usually means a longer search term. It can take a few goes to get this right, but it is time well spent.
7. Scroll back up to the top of the site and now enter your website address and that of key competitors and Google will scrape the sites and pull out all the keywords, so review for additional suggestions.
8. Select and export the keywords that you want to use.
9. Google your selected keywords one by one and see what content appears - how can you improve on what's out there? This is a great starting point for content creation.

Three big social media mistakes to avoid

> "Never interrupt your enemy when he is making a mistake."
>
> **Napoleon Bonaparte**

GET TO GRIPS WITH SOCIAL MEDIA

When you look at all the tools and channels of communication available to you, there has never been a better time to be in business with a restricted budget. The access to your target audience that YouTube, Facebook, Twitter, Google+ and myriad other social sites give you is unprecedented. With all the content you are now going to start to create, you can create huge amounts of word of mouth for a relatively small cost. But, you have to cut through the clutter.

Lots of small business owners believe you need to be technically savvy to be good at social media. This is just not true. There are some guiding principles that can help you to quickly become an expert, so if the only Java you know is a type of coffee, you will still be ok. If you've already dipped your toe into social media and are not getting the results you wanted, then make sure you are not making the mistakes outlined below.

First things first, have you thought about the role that social media plays in your marketing strategy? It's usually viewed as the inexpensive way to broaden reach and generate advocacy. This is often followed with disappointment, as the video didn't "go viral", the blog post only got three comments and Twitter followers and Facebook fans are dribbling in and not beating down the door. What keeps going wrong? There are three big mistakes that hold most business owners back.

1. It's a one way dialogue

The idea is to start a conversation, not a monologue. People always seem to forget that they are connecting with other human beings when interacting on social media sites. You need to create a conversation, not shout about your latest deal. Take a look back at your posts, what percentage are re-tweeted, replied to or shared? If it is less than 10% you really need to rethink your strategy. If it's about 20%, you're doing ok, but you should aim for a minimum of 30%. It's not about the size of your following, it's how engaged they are with what you have to say.

2. Social media is a "bolt-on"

Social media is not and never should be a bolt-on to the rest of your marketing. As with any other channel, it should have clear business goals, such as increasing leads, growing awareness, driving up loyalty, improving conversions, lowering customer service costs. All too often business owners feel they have to engage with social media because their competitors are, which leads to dabbling rather than the creation of a focused strategy. I see this a lot.

3. Low expectations

As social media is still a fairly new channel, uncertainty surrounds how you value a tweet, a like a share or a re-tweet. It's therefore seen as an experiment and, as it's "free", it comes with little expectation. This leads to a scatter gun approach, as opposed to a well thought through strategy with clear objectives and deliverables. Once you get clear on your objectives for social media, the value of each interaction becomes a lot clearer.

Social media can play a really powerful role in your business, as it's your opportunity to engage, influence and activate a loyal following. However, first you need to gain their trust and to do this you need to demonstrate value. Ask yourself why your target audience would sign up to your social media updates? What do they want from you?

ExactTarget's study, "The UK social profile", revealed that the primary reason consumers like a brand's Facebook page, or follow them on Twitter is to gain access to discounts and deals. The second reason is to receive free stuff, downloads, giveaways, followed by a desire to stay informed about the company's activities and to get updates on future products. So if deals are all you give your fans and followers, you are cheapening your relationship. They are connecting with you as they also want to know more about what you're up to and that's easy content to create. In addition, involve your customers and prospects in your decision making, every now and then ask their opinion and prove that you listen by implementing their ideas and letting them know that you have. It will have a positive impact on sales.

Many companies view social media as another potential sales channel and after pumping out numerous promotional tweets and updates they become frustrated with the lack of response. It simply doesn't work that way. If every time I called my clients, I tried to sell them something, they wouldn't be my clients for very long. It works the same in the online world. Social media is, by definition, social, so don't forget that you need to have a conversation and build a relationship. You also need to put a strategy in place to move people from passive "friends" to paying customers which is the subject of the next chapter.

ACTION

- ❏ What is the role for social media in your business? List out what you want to achieve through each channel on which you have a presence.

- ❏ Review each of your social media channels, how much interaction do you get from your readers? What type of content creates the most interest?

- ❏ If you have a YouTube channel which videos have the most views? Review the titles and tags on each to ensure they correspond with your keyword list.

- ❏ Check out your competitors' social media sites, do they get more or less interaction from their followers? Identify the content that generates the most engagement.

How to create a social media strategy

> "Nobody cares how much you know, until
> they know how much you care."
> **Roosevelt**

Now you have set your objectives for social media, it's time to create a strategy.

GETTING STARTED

Before getting started in social media there are some practical considerations for your business that you need to figure out first. There is nothing worse than a company launching into the social media space with great intent only to discover that they don't have the resources to manage the relationships. Consider who will manage the day to day, you, your team, or someone outside the company? If you are outsourcing, consider creating social media guidelines that govern the type of content shared and how to respond to potential issues. When it comes to user generated content, it's important to think about moderation guidelines for what gets approved or refused. You can't plan for every eventuality in social media, but it helps to have thought through a few scenarios first.

STEP ONE: DISCOVER

Even if you already have a presence on social media it's still important to analyse the strengths and weaknesses of each of the different channels, as you don't have to have a presence on every one, just those that deliver results in your industry. Look at what your competitors are doing, where is their social reach (the volume of fans, followers, views) the greatest? When starting out, prioritise a presence on these sites to begin with. Record the type of content that creates conversation on their sites; what are people responding to positively? What gets ignored? This will help you with your content strategy later.

STEP TWO: LISTEN

The reason we have two ears and one mouth is because it's twice as important to listen as to talk. That's why step two is one of the most important steps. What are people already saying about your brand and about you? If you're not listening, you do not have a chance to defend yourself when criticised, or to amplify positive feedback. There are numerous listening tools on the market, the more sophisticated are paid such as Radian6 and Sysomos, they have products that allow you to track conversations happening in blogs, social networks, news sites and more. For a less sophisticated, but still effective solution that is free try HootSuite, which allows you to set up searches on keywords, although it is limited to Twitter. To listen in to mentions elsewhere, set up keyword alerts on Google Alerts and Social Mention, they are both free and send updates to your inbox linking to the content each time your keywords are published. List out your brand and product names, plus those of your competitors as this can be a source of competitive insight if they are getting a lot of positive or negative feedback.

STEP THREE: ENGAGE

The conversations that you listened in to about your brand and your competitors in the listening phase, coupled with the type of content that engages your target that you identified in the discovery phase, will help shape your engagement strategy. Whilst the next chapter covers content creation in greater detail, let's cover a few guiding principles.

Your fans and followers are hot prospects

They have actively connected with you and want to buy from you. Sharing testimonials and positive comments is a great way to build credibility and as a result, increase take up of your promotions and deals.

Create conversations that show that you care.

End posts with questions that demand a response, post tweets in the same way. Ask for feedback, ideas, in-put; your social media sites are a great way to get some quick research done. A local cafe thinking of starting a loyalty programme asked for feedback on the type of rewards customers wanted. Because they were involved in the creation of the loyalty programme, take up was significantly higher than expected. A greeting card designer regularly posts her new designs and asks customers which they like the most. This also gives her a great story to tell the retail buyers to help to sell her designs to large department stores.

Respond quickly

A speedy response is critical on social media, particularly if there is a problem. If you can't resolve it quickly, then let people know that you're working on finding a solution. Communication is key.

Run promotions

Remember that your customers connect with you across social media, as they want to be the first to hear about promotions and offers, so consider seeding new promotions before they happen, to create excitement. Two weeks in advance you could tweet about an amazing promotion that you are putting together and tell people to watch out for it on a particular day. If you're choosing between prizes for a competition, simply ask your fans and followers for their opinions, they will love to tell you. Just make sure that you listen and act on their input.

How often should you tweet, post and blog?

I'm always asked this, but there is no hard and fast rule. Each channel requires different frequencies and has different types of content. People tweet far more than they blog due to the brevity. It also depends on how many people you have to manage your social media activity. I tend to tweet a minimum of three times a day and post to Facebook about the same, in addition I respond to comments and tweets. I go through my content marketing strategy in more detail in the next chapter. In an ideal world it would be great to be able to respond to every tweet and comment as soon as it comes in, but for most companies, this is just not feasible. Do what you can, establish a frequency that works for you and when it becomes more than you can handle, outsource it. There is a danger that social media activity will swallow you up whole if you're not careful. It's always good to share the responsibility with a wider team, or ideally have a dedicated resource.

When it comes to blogging, again there are no hard and fast rules, as it very much depends on your content and your objective for the blog. You might write just one long blog post a month, but the content remains relevant for years and becomes an ongoing source of traffic via search engines. Alternatively you could write a couple of shorter posts a week, it's really a question of resources, but whatever your approach, you need to deliver high quality, engaging content.

STEP FOUR: TRACK & EVALUATE

What you track and evaluate depends on the objectives of your social media activity, but it's important that social media metrics link to your broader business objectives. It's also important to analyse your success metrics on a regular basis. At the end of every campaign, or the end of every month, whichever comes first, conduct a post analysis, identify what worked, what didn't and what you will do differently next time. Ensure that at a minimum your evaluation is monthly.

This is not an exhaustive list, but following are examples of what you could track:

Social Reach

- ❑ Growth in fans, followers, subscribers, views.
- ❑ Monitor unsubscribe rates to identify trends and causes.
- ❑ Increase in social mentions - positive and negative.

Social Engagement

- ❑ Percentage of fans / followers / subscribers who share content on each site.
- ❑ Time of day your content gets highest levels of engagement.
- ❑ YouTube views, comments and ratings.
- ❑ The type of content that gets shared the most:
  - Track comments / re-tweets / shares / likes.

Social Results

- ❑ Opt-in rates to promotions by channel:
  - Monitor whether your blog delivers a higher promotional uptake versus Twitter, Facebook, Google+.
  - What offers spread like wildfire and which bomb?
- ❑ Increased website traffic generated by social media:
  - Track traffic volume by site (this is easily done on Google Analytics, just make sure that you review it)
- ❑ Conversions:
  - If you have an e-commerce site, set up goal tracking in Google Analytics to track which channel (Facebook, Twitter, Google+ or others) drives the greatest volume of sales. There are numerous tutorials available online to help you set up goal tracking, so I won't go into it here. Just "Google":'Google analytics goal tracking set up" and take your pick.
  - Track which social site drives the greatest number of sign-ups to your database, this can also be set-up using Google's goal tracking.
- ❑ Percentage of customers per social network; how many of your Facebook fans or Twitter followers turn into paying

customers? To identify this you need to set up conversion tracking as outlined above, you can then track growth month by month.

If you don't sell your products or services online, your social results might be focused on the volume of customer service requests satisfied through social media versus other channels, you can then evaluate the contribution to lower customer service costs over time.

SUMMARY

Whatever your goals and objectives, the regular tracking and evaluation of activity enables you to identify trends; once you know the type of content that delivers the highest levels of engagement, you can create more of the same. This kind of analysis is what turns you from being an amateur to a professional and will ensure your social media success. Following these four steps gives you a strategic framework for integrating social media campaigns into your business. How you approach social media needs to be as well thought through as your communications in offline channels, as it is an integral and important part of your communication strategy.

ACTION

- ❏ Get clear on who is responsible for managing your social media activity and put guidelines in place around rules of engagement.

- ❏ Identify the strengths and weaknesses of each social media channel for your sector. Where are your competitors? More importantly, where are your consumers spending most of their time?

- ❏ Set up Google Alerts and Social Mentions for your brand, you and your competitors.

- ❏ Agree the key metrics that you will track and evaluate on an ongoing basis.

How to never run out of something to say on social media

"If you fail to plan, you are planning to fail."
Benjamin Franklin

Just because you sign up to Facebook, Twitter, Google+ or Pinterest does not mean that the gates are open and fans and followers will come flooding in. You need a strategy; you need to plan both a content and an "attraction" strategy to build and grow your following on an on-going basis.

CREATING A MESSAGING STRATEGY

As with every aspect of your marketing, you need to have a strategic approach to your content. At the start of each month I plan and write my social media content for the next four weeks and I usually take about half a day to do this. Note that here, I am referring to short content only, so posts and tweets, not blogs or articles. Short content can be uploaded in bulk to an online social media management tool, and delivered at scheduled intervals. I have listed example automated tools below. This is not the only content that I will share, it is the minimum, I then add in promotions, blogs and articles throughout the month, as well as engage one to one with fans and followers, re-tweeting, re-posting and commenting. What I like most about this upfront planning, is that if I end up being too busy to do additional posts or tweets during the month, I am still publishing content week in, week out and this builds my profile as a thought leader on my topics.

Planning in advance also enables you to think strategically about your content. What you share positions you within your niche, so plan your content around keywords you want to be known for and that are relevant to your target audience.

Step 1: How many tweets / posts....?

Begin by deciding the number of tweets and posts you want to send each day, a good start point is three on each social network.

Step 2: What is the timescale of your plan?

I plan four weeks ahead. Decide how much time you have to devote to planning and writing, a couple of hours a fortnight, might be more manageable, as it takes me half a day to write all my short content for the month.

Step 3: Decide on your keywords

Decide on four topics you want to be seen as an expert and authority on, one for each week of the month, four of my topics are marketing, branding, advertising and entrepreneurship. Then choose three keywords for each topic, one for each post or tweet you will send out each day.

	1	2	3	4
Topics	**Marketing**	**Branding**	**Advertising**	**Entrepreneurship**
Keywords	Positioning	Brand Identity	Social Media	Mentors
	Strategy	Brand Design	Research	Business Advice
	Consumer	Personal Branding	SEO	Business Plan

You then need to generate seven tweets or posts for each keyword, one for each day of the week. I create the actual tweets and posts in an excel spreadsheet and then mix the topics up throughout the week, but you might prefer the theme for each week to be your topic, which is just fine. I prefer to create separate content for Facebook and Twitter rather than auto-tweet what gets posted to Facebook. I think automating content in this way is lazy, as hashtags don't work in Facebook and using the @ sign to link a friend into a Facebook post does not work in Twitter. If you want to post the same content just re-write it. Following this approach means you need to generate eighty-four bits of content for each social media site:

7 days x 3 tweets x 4 topics = 84

7 days x 3 Facebook posts x 4 topics = 84

This sounds a lot, but step 4 will make you realise it's easier than you think.

Step 4: Decide on the type of content

Creating content on twelve keywords might sound like a lot of work, but you can make it easy for yourself by varying the type of content you create. Consider the following variations:

- ❑ Ask questions to get feedback.
- ❑ Share a famous quote on your topic.
- ❑ Create a survey or poll (great way to research ideas for longer form content).
- ❑ Give a piece of advice or a business tip.
- ❑ Link to "evergreen" content on your blog. This is content that doesn't date and remains relevant for a long time, perhaps even, forever.
- ❑ Comment on third-party research studies.
- ❑ Share photos / videos.
- ❑ Link to presentations on Slideshare, they don't have to be yours.
- ❑ Share fun stuff on your topic to make people laugh.
- ❑ Make provocative statements to start a discussion.

Leverage the myriad tools available online, consider Facebook polls, Twitpic, Twitvid, Twtpoll. If you use three different content forms to deliver your key messages on each site, you will be surprised at how quickly you complete this task.

> Tip: When you complete the research phase of your social media strategy you will identify the type of content that goes viral in your niche, so make sure your keywords are also hitting topics of interest to your niche.

Step 5: Schedule your content

There are a number of tools available that allow you to schedule your content in advance, HootSuite and BufferApp are two I recommend, though BufferApp is my preferred. You need to schedule your valuable content at peak times, but not all at once. When conducting your research, you should note the time of day that most content gets shared, as well as the best type of content. If you use BufferApp it analyses your Twitter and Facebook sites and schedules your posts at the most effective times. Note that at the time of writing it is not yet enabled for Google+.

> Tip: One of the key strengths of social media is being able to respond in real time to tweets and comments, but scheduling content in advance means that you're not there, so try and find time to check in each day and respond to conversations.

ACTION

❑ Decide on the social media networks to which you want to commit. You don't have to have a presence on all of them, just select those that your target audience uses the most.

❑ Follow steps one to five and monitor the type of content that creates a conversation.

How to explode your Facebook following

> "How can you squander even one more day not taking advantage of the greatest shifts of our generation? How dare you settle for less when the world has made it so easy for you to be remarkable?"
> **Seth Godin**

GROWING FANS ON FACEBOOK

There are a number of creative ways to grow your fans, this is by no means an exhaustive list, but it is a good start.

Invite friends

As soon as your page is completed, invite your Facebook friends via the invite tab.

Add Facebook social plug-ins to your website

There are a number of plug-ins available that you can embed onto your website. The "Like" box widget is particularly effective, as it displays your current fan page stream and a selection of fans. If the person browsing your website is currently logged into Facebook, it will mention which of their friends are fans, which has a huge impact on increasing likes. To further drive up "likes" add a call to action above the box that encourages fans to click the "like" button.

Tell your email subscribers that your page is live

There are huge benefits to letting your whole database know that your Facebook page is live, because when your fans and followers "like" your page, or comment on or "like" your posts, it immediately gets posted to their wall and all of their friends get to see it. Same goes for Twitter; if someone re-tweets your post, then it has the potential to be seen by all of their followers. Social media sites are a great way to build awareness of your brand, fast.

So, when you launch your Facebook page, mail your email subscribers and incentivise them to join you by telling them that this is where you will share exclusive content, promotional deals, more regular updates and more.

Add a link to your email sign off

Add a link at the bottom of every email to your Facebook fan page (and any other social media sites). If you use web-based mail then WiseStamp have an easy way of adding all social media channels to your signature. If not, then you can just write in the url.

Use the "share" button

The "Share" button is found in the drop down box on the right hand side of your page and allows you to post a comment to your personal timeline. Add a few lines about all the great content you're sharing and encourage people to become your fans.

Post photos of events

If you hold events, take lots of photos and encourage your fans to tag themselves when you upload them as this will push out to their wall and news feeds for all their friends to see. Pictures are also much more noticeable in the newsfeed, so they have the potential to drive greater interest.

Sign up fans via SMS

You can get people to become your fans via SMS, which is great at live events! Ask people to send a text message to 32665 (FBOOK) and to type: like yourusername

Note that they need to first have a verified mobile number on their account and you need to have at least twenty-five fans and have claimed your username. http://facebook.com/username.

Use the @ tag

Write a personal status update telling your friends what you've been up to on your Facebook Page, or share more content and include the "@ tag" in the update to create a hyperlink to your fan page. As you type the @ and the start of your page name, a list of options appear and you can just select your page name.

Facebook promotions

Facebook offers promoted posts and sponsored stories which are a very effective way of quickly driving up "likes" to your page.

Promote offline

If you have a physical location you can encourage sign-up to your Facebook page through strategically positioned posters or signs. Consider incentivising an immediate sign-up by offering some kind of instant reward if they show your staff that they have liked your page.

You can also add a link to your page on advertising, business cards, menus, posters, business stationery and even packaging. Make sure that you have claimed your name, so that the URL is easy to enter.

ACTION

❑ If your page is already live, then commit to using two of the above strategies in the next seven days.

❑ Monitor the increase in fans as you trial each strategy.

How to explode your Twitter following

> "Conversations among the members of your marketplace happen whether you like it or not. Good marketing encourages the right sort of conversations."
> **Seth Godin**

GROWING FOLLOWERS ON TWITTER

As with Facebook, there are so many ways to grow your Twitter followers, but here are a few tried and tested strategies.

Complete your profile

No one wants to connect with a faceless Twitter account, so make sure you complete your bio and add a photo. When it comes to your Twitter ID, it's a good idea to use your name, rather than just your brand, as it's more personal.

Look for people you already know

A no-brainer, but often forgotten. Click on the "Find Friends" tab and select your email account. This is limited to web based emails, but there is a way around this. Set up a Gmail account and export your contacts from your current email provider and import them into your new Gmail account. You can then go back to Twitter and pull them in. You might find lots of your clients and customers are already on Twitter.

Twijazzle your blog or website

Twitter offer buttons and widgets that you can add to your website to encourage people to sign up to your Twitter account. They range from buttons showing the number of followers to live streams of your tweets. To create yours go to: www.twitter.com/logo

Tweet regularly at peak times

When is your Twitter stream the noisiest? This is a high traffic time and a great time to tweet as your audience is there. There are a number of tools that can help you to identify the peak times on your account, but here are the two I find most useful:

BufferApp: I've already mentioned this tool, it enables you to schedule tweets in advance and it auto selects the most effective times to tweet on your account. It also gives basic analytics, such as reach, ReTweets and clicks.

Timely: Is a tool that analyses your tweets and helps you to identify the best times to tweet for maximum impact. However, it doesn't let you control the times or schedule tweets days in advance. You load up the tweets and Timely sends them out throughout the day based on the times and performance of past tweets.

Listen

You need to tune in to the conversations happening on Twitter in your niche. Twilert is a great tool that enables you do to just that, it's essentially Google Alerts for Twitter. You can set up searches on your keywords and competitors and they are emailed to you daily. The advanced options allow you to track the location of who sends/receives a tweet, which is useful for local businesses.

Use Hashtags (#)

Hashtags group together tweets on the same subject, so when someone clicks on a hashtag they go straight to a page showing all the recent tweets on that subject. It's great for conferences, as not only does it gather the comments together, but it also gives those who can't attend the event a running commentary. If a lot of people use a hashtag at the same time it can become one of Twitter's trending topics, these are the big news stories on Twitter at any one time. Once you become a trending topic it can become a self-fulfilling prophecy, as lots of people click on the trending topics to find out what's going on and to join the conversation. I use hashtags to broaden the visibility of my tweets and regularly add #branding, #marketing or #SME to the end of my tweets, as these tags are followed by a relevant audience who then start to follow me. It's important to only use a hashtag when it is relevant, otherwise you will come across as a spammer. A few years ago, Habitat got into hot water for using a "trending topic" hashtag in unrelated tweets. Habitat angered a number of people by spamming the conversations around the Iranian protests, by using the hashtag in a promotional tweet. Habitat also used #iphone and #Apple hashtags in the wake of Apple's iphone 3GS launch. Twitter users reacted very negatively to the publicity stunt:

> Caramboo: "Just read about your hashtag abuses, you utter scumbags, I'll never visit your shop again"

> Brownbare: "Naughty, money-grabbing furniture outlet. Bad bad bad. Now I'm glad I can't afford your overpriced IKEA replicas"

Habitat hastily apologised and promised it wouldn't happen again, but the damage was done and they were all over the news for the wrong reasons.

There are lots of different ways to identify hashtags on relevant topics, but here are the two resources I use:

Twubs: Twubs are Twitter groups built around content. The site aggregates the tweets and categorises them so they are easier to find. It also adds video and photos and has a useful search function. You can also register your hashtag there, so you can start your own trending topic.

Hashtags.org: This tracks the frequency a hashtag is used on Twitter and helps you to understand the meaning behind the tag. It also lets you see trends in their use over time.

Use #FollowFriday

Follow Friday is a weekly international event created by Micha Baldwin at the start of 2009. It stemmed from the idea that if you didn't know who to follow you would most likely ask your friends for recommendations and follow their suggestions, which is exactly how #FollowFriday began. The idea is to think of interesting people that you know on Twitter and suggest them to your followers each Friday. It's "feel good" karma and gives you an extra tweet or two a week.

Search for people

It's completely normal to follow people you have never met, in fact it's encouraged. You can start by looking for people with similar interests, jobs, hobbies, people who are experts in your field, or even in subjects you know nothing about, but want to. There are two to help you search:

Twitter.com/search: Very easy to use and a great start point

WeFollow.com: This is the Twitter people directory, you can also add yourself and search for the most prolific twitters in relevant categories to your business.

Engage in conversation

Be human and get involved in conversations, re-tweet posts you find interesting, comment on others, ask questions, garner opinions - just get connecting. It's a great feeling to promote one of your followers, instead of yourself and it starts a dialogue.

Follow those who follow you

If someone follows you, they are interested in what you have to say, so follow them back if their bio interests you. Be warned though, this can become overwhelming, as when you start to have a large following your Twitter stream becomes very crowded and you end up missing important tweets. To avoid this, create lists of the key people you want to keep up with, this assigns all of their tweets to one stream and makes it much easier to manage. I have lists for different topics - branding experts, entrepreneurs, clients, journalists and scan these each day to keep up to date.

Add your Twitter ID to your email sign off

As with Facebook, include a "follow me on Twitter" sign off on your emails and if you post on blogs and forums you can also add it to the end of your posts.

Vary your content

If you tweet great content, it will get shared, so as I outlined earlier, vary what and how you share your thoughts and ideas. Combine text based tweets with video, photos, polls, or even the latest tunes you're listening to. As Twitter doesn't have these functions built in, lots of third party services have sprung up. Following are the ones I use, but a quick Google search will give you a whole lot more.

Twitpics: This hugely popular service lets you tweet photos or videos from your phone, on the site or via email. Easy and instant.

song.ly: This service is integrated with Twitter, so you simply search for an artist or track and press the tweet button which sends you off to Twitter and pre-populates the tweet for you with shortened URL. Useful as listeners don't need to download the song to listen, as it plays in their browser.

twtpoll.com: Easily create polls and post them to Twitter and Facebook, you can also post the results to your blog once they're in. A free or paid service depending on your usage needs.

ACTION

- ❑ If you already have a Twitter account then select two attraction strategies you haven't used and commit to executing them in the next seven days.

- ❑ Monitor the increase in followers as you trial each strategy.

Getting to grips with Google+

"Be part of the party/conversation/
network before you need anything from
anyone."
Jeremiah Owyang

Despite being the new kid on the block in the social media world, Google+ has already got more than 100 million[9] active users. I have to say, it isn't that easy to understand at first, as it has a lot of features with the potential to confuse. However, it is worth getting your head around, as it's here to stay and is rapidly taking online search in a whole new direction. At the start of 2012, Google rolled out "search plus your world", which personalises the results from your contacts, these could be shared posts, images or pages that have been given a +1 by your contacts or even pages on Google+ that you are not connected to. This is a really interesting move, as people really trust recommendations from known contacts. However, Google heavily favours its own content in search engines, so if you are not using Google's tools, you are significantly less likely to show up. Google denies this, but just take a look for yourself.

Google+ is essentially a collection of different social products:

❑ **Home** - your news stream.

❑ **Circles** - a tool to organise your friends and search for people.

❑ **Explore** - this shows you what is currently trending on Google+.

9   http://uk.reuters.com/article/2012/04/05/us-google-idUKBRE83418220120405

- ❑ **Hangouts** - a video chat service.

- ❑ **Events** - a tool to create events or search and browse for public events.

- ❑ **Photos** - a photo album product that enables you to instantly upload your photos via the Google+ app.

- ❑ **Games** - search for and play a number of third party games using the directory.

- ❑ **Pages** - a way to use Google+ for your business.

The best way to get your head around it is simply to roll your sleeves up and get stuck in by playing around. Once you have got to grips with the basics, there are some tips to grow your following.

ATTRACTION STRATEGY

1. Fill out your bio

Fill out your "about" page as much as possible, as Google is first and foremost a search engine and Google will use this information to help other people to connect with you by featuring you in search results on your keywords. A great way to see if your profile represents you in the way you want it to is to copy your "about" section and paste it into a word cloud tool like Wordle or Tag Crowd, this will highlight the dominant keywords.

Choose your avatar, your key photo, wisely. This is the first thing that people will see. Be human, don't put a logo here, show your face. It hopefully goes without saying that a photo of you looking hammered or semi-naked is a no, but just in case, I have spelled it out!

The scrapbook refers to the five photos below your avatar, you can put your logo here if you want to, or photos of your products, your team or your events, whatever is relevant. You can have more than five photos, but five feature on your profile.

If you need to change the order go to Picasa and click on the Scrapbook folder to rearrange them.

Create a tagline that reflects what you do and who you are. You have a limited space, so choose your words wisely and make it interesting. What you say here will be a key determinant of whether people connect with you or not.

Make sure you also add the links to your other social profiles in the "other profiles" section.

2. Connect with your friends

The wider your circles, the further your content reaches. Use the "find your friends" link on the right hand side to see who is already on Google+ and then invite those who are not.

3. Set up a Google+ page for business

These are Google's version of Facebook pages and you have all the same functionalities; you can build followers, upload photos and share your thoughts. The difference is that users +1 a page to show their interest. If users search for your brand with the + sign, it will go directly to this page.

4. Create circles

Circles are a way of separating your friends so you can manage how you share your content. You can create as many, or as few circles as you want, but don't create too many, as it defeats the purpose of the segmentation. Other people can't see your circles unless you share them, so you can give them any nicknames you like. Create circles that are relevant to your business, put yourself inside and then share them, it's a great way to gain followers.

5. Search for people

Use the search function to find people with similar interests and hobbies and add them to your circles.

6. Import other people's circles

There is an option to import other people's circles when they share them, you can either incorporate them into your own circles, or create new ones. You can either wait until their post shows up in your stream, or you can search on the term "shared a circle with you" and you will get the list of those who have. You can further refine the search by adding additional keywords.

7. Get engaged

When you follow people, +1 their posts, comment on them and share them with other circles, you will be rewarded with reciprocation. Make sure that you also respond to comments on your posts if they require answers.

8. Use the + sign

When you mention people, use the + sign in the same way you use the @ sign on Facebook; it will make you more visible.

9. Start a hangout

Hangouts are a form of video broadcasting for up to ten people at one time. You can easily set them up and invite people. You can then share screens, mute people, use a sketchpad to doodle with participants, collaborate on or present a Google doc and more. When the Hangout is over, Google connects you to You-Tube and you have a full length, private recording of it. There are also a number of free tools available to record your hangouts and I have put these in the resources box below.

You can also dial people into your Hangout, so whilst they won't have the video function, they can still participate in the broadcast. You can also create a hangout from a status update, so instead of comments going back and forth you can connect in person.

10. Create interesting content

As with anywhere else online, create content that people want to share. Don't talk about how amazing your products and services are, instead share something of value with your community that helps them in some way. When you share content, your connections can then re-share it and it has the potential to go viral across your network and beyond, unless you "disable re-share" that is.

ACTION

- ❑ If you don't yet have a presence on Google+, take a look, as it is here to stay and the personalised search functions will have a big impact over time.

- ❑ If you already have a presence, is your home page working hard for you? Does your avatar show you in a favourable light? Could your tagline be more effective?

- ❑ Focus on growing your circles, as the more circles in which you show up, the wider your content reaches.

RESOURCES

Here are some useful free tools to record your Hangouts, or any other screen recordings.

ScreenCastle

This records the entire screen, or you can control the size of the recording. It starts from the moment you hit record until your Hangout is complete and the duration is unlimited. You then have to upload the recording to their site. To share the video you can send a direct link or embed the code on your site.

Screencast-O-Matic

What I like about this software is the ability to resize the window to fit your recording, so it is ideal for Hangouts. It's also incredibly simple to use. However, on the free version you are limited to fifteen minute recordings and you have a Screencast-O-Matic logo at the bottom of your video. It's inexpensive to get the Pro version which means that you are limited only by your local disk space.

Pixetell

Download the software and when you're ready to record you quite simply hit the record button and it records your screen and then shrinks down to a small timer, opening back up again when you stop the recording. You can upload directly to YouTube or export in a number of file formats. It's a great tool, but it doesn't work for Mac's.

BB Flashback Express

This is for Windows only and is a free download from Blue-berry software. What's great about this tool is the ability to select whether it records your whole screen or just a browser window, so it is great for Hangouts. It comes with basic edit options and you can upload directly to YouTube or export the video, though only as flash or AVI.

If you are interested in a paid version then Screenflow for Mac and Camtasia for PC are both excellent.

Social media disasters and how to avoid them

> "A person who never made a mistake
> never tried anything new."
> **Albert Einstein**

WHY YOU NEED TO BE BOTH HONEST AND TRANSPARENT AS A BUSINESS

As you raise your profile, the way that you run and manage your business will come under greater scrutiny. Your brand is your reputation and you need to take great care of it. In today's hyper connected society, you cannot sweep anything under the carpet, hoping that no one will notice, as social media has amplified transparency. The online space is defined by its openness and its immediacy and anyone, including your customers, can communicate with you and the rest of the world in an instant. For many, this is a frightening reality, as it demands new levels of openness and many businesses are just not prepared. Transparency is never more important than when something has gone wrong. When the world is "on" 24/7, information gets out and lives on...and on. Social media networks, in particular Twitter and YouTube offer consumers instant, powerful ways to strike out and vilify with often devastating consequences. A number of brands have learned this the hard way.

United Airlines - Guitar Gate!

When United Airlines broke musician Dave Carroll's treasured Taylor guitar and refused to take responsibility he decided to take revenge. He believed the damage was caused by rough handling, as while waiting to get off the plane he heard a customer exclaim: "My God, they're throwing guitars out there."

When Dave's guitar came through baggage reclaim, despite its hard case, it was badly damaged and United Airlines, for almost a year, refused to cover the repair costs of $1,200. Dave then embarked upon a very creative revenge. He composed a song called "United Breaks Guitars" and posted it on YouTube, it gave the little known Canadian band an instant hit, as the catchy tune went viral and got almost 4 million views in ten days on YouTube. Despite being posted over two years ago, views are still increasing and new comments appear every single day. United's nightmare lives on and on.

You can watch the video here: www.jacquelinebiggs.com/United

Guitar-gate had devastating consequences for United. The company lost "10%[10] of their share value – a massive $180 million". In contrast, Dave and his band soared  to stardom and their track became the 20th best selling track on iTunes in Canada. Taylor guitars offered him a new guitar and Dave found himself appearing on American breakfast shows while his group's album started to fly off the shelves for the first time ever. This clearly demonstrates how the balance of power has shifted, social media has given everyone new and incredibly powerful tools to share displeasure, fast. United Airlines tried to put on a brave face and admitted its mistake on Twitter and announced that it would donate $3,000 to a music charity, but too little too late. United now use the video for training purposes to ensure all customers receive better service from the company in future. That is clearly the least that they can do.

10   http://www.dailymail.co.uk/news/article-1201671/Singer-Dave-Carroll-pens-YouTube-hit-United-Airlines-breaks-guitar--shares-plunge-10.html

Domino's Pizza's Disaster

Bad publicity can unfortunately also come via staff members and Domino's Pizza learnt this lesson the hard way. Two, now former, employees of Domino's in the USA, videoed themselves doing some pretty unspeakable, unhygienic things to the pizzas they were preparing.

It confirms the fear of what could go on behind the closed doors of a restaurant. Clearly finding their antics hilarious, they then posted the video on YouTube. The video was picked up and covered by US blog, The Consumerist. It then got quickly embedded in dozens of other blogs, tweeted across Twitter feeds and spread like wildfire across Facebook. The pace of the exposure was phenomenal, it quickly went global, being picked up by the BBC, SKY and other channels. The effect was immediate. The New York Times reported how a YouGov poll showed that consumers' perception of Domino's went from positive to negative overnight.

However, Domino's response was poor and slow; it comprised a comment on the initial blog post, failing to address the now hundreds of others. Later an official statement was issued on the Domino's website to its "valued customers". The employees were tracked down and fired, but the damage had been done. The video reached one million views before it was taken down with the notice:

> "This video is no longer available due to a copyright claim by Kristy Hammonds."

Kristy was one of the two employees. News travels fast, especially when it's bad. As a spokesperson for Domino's rightly said:

"In the course of one three-minute video, two idiots can attempt to unravel everything that is great about the brand."

Domino's did finally remedy the situation a few days later. Patrick Doyle, the President, issued a video apology and outlined what they were going to do. It was an appropriate direct response, but it was too late and it received significantly less views. Domino's then started a Twitter account, realising the importance of demonstrating that they are paying attention and listening to the many voices and concerns of their customers.

Again we see too little too late; if Domino's had had the appropriate listening tools in place, their response would have been a lot quicker. Loyal customers alerted them to the issues, but they were slow to pick this up, as they were yet to have a presence on Twitter and had clearly not set up any online alerts.

Dell Computers

Often heralded as a social media success story, everything wasn't always rosy for Dell in the online world. In 2005 a blogger called Jeff Jervis proved how easy it could be to topple a huge brand with his "Dell Hell" campaign. After buying a computer that was "a lemon" and receiving no customer service he decided to blog about his experience and no one at Dell was listening. It went viral....quickly. Reader after reader left comments about their Dell Hell and the saga snowballed. Despite emailing Dell repeatedly through their various online  channels, Jeff got no response. Only when he sent an email to the chief marketing officer and US vice president did he finally get a reply. He was offered a new machine, which he refused, instead switching to an Apple mac. As he sent his PC back he blogged an open letter to Dell with a few words of advice. Although written in 2005 and the social media landscape has changed significantly since, his points are still relevant today.

Following is a shortened excerpt, but you can find the full blog post here: www.jacquelinebiggs.com/Dell

---

Big mistakes

So allow me to give you some friendly and free advice about these blog things. You can pay for more.

- ❏ **Read blogs** at Technorati.com or Icerocket.com, Google and Bloglines search for what people say about your brand. Don't think of bloggers as strange beasts blathering, but as people, just customers. Beats any focus group.

- ❏ **Talk with your consumers.** A Dell PR executive told blogger and Houston Chronicle columnist Dwight Silverman that the company's blog policy was, in Silverman's words, "look, don't touch". How insulting: You ignore your customers. How much better it would be to ask their advice. Beats any consultant.

- ❏ **Blog.** If execs at Microsoft, Sun, and even GM can, you can. Show that you are open and unafraid to engage your public. Beats PR.

- ❏ **Listen** to all your bad press and bad blog PR and consumer dissatisfaction and falling stock price and to the failure of your low-price strategy and use that blog to admit that you have a problem. Then show us how you are going to improve quality and let us help. Make better computers and hire customer service people who serve customers.

The impact of this saga was catastrophic for Dell, their customer satisfaction rating, market share, and share price in the US all declined. Needless to say their policy on blogging changed dramatically shortly afterwards and today Dell is a model social media citizen.

A tough lesson to learn, but be glad it is Dell and not you. Whether you are a large or small company, I can't stress enough the importance of being aware of the conversations that are happening about you and your brand. If Dell had been tuned in, the outcome could have been very different.

HOW SHOULD YOU RESPOND TO A PR NIGHTMARE?

❑ **Get the facts:** Quickly get to grips with the situation and decide on how you will communicate your response to consumers and the press.

❑ **Fast:** Speed of response is critical in a crisis. Unfortunately Domino's were alerted late and the damage was done before they even knew the crisis had hit.

❑ **Publicly:** Posting an apology on a corporate website just for "valued customers" does not address the scale of the problem. It needs to be tackled head on; it won't just go away!

❑ **Proactively:** Call the top twenty-five journalists who cover your sector and tell them the story and your response.

❑ **Repeatedly:** Release on-going updates, ideally hourly on Twitter, stating what you are doing to address the situation.

❑ **Positively:** Identify what you can do to try and get some positive PR. It might well be too little too late, but something is always better than nothing

ACTION

❑ If someone wants to complain, is it easy to get in contact with you? Make sure any contact forms on your website go to regularly checked email addresses, as even twenty-four hours can have devastating consequences.

❑ What does your social media presence say about your brand? How are you using it? Are you listening, as well as talking?

❑ If you haven't yet set up social alerts, please do it today.

Great social media examples

"Our head of social media is the customer."
McDonald's

Whilst disasters do happen, there are also some amazing success stories of companies big and small. Big brands might have big budgets and a team of people helping them to manage multiple outposts, but you can still learn a great deal about the ingredients to a successful social media campaign. Let's have a look at a few success stories.

ZAPPOS

The American online shoe and clothing retailer excels at micro blogging and is one of the great social media success stories. In an earlier chapter, I outlined how the heart of Zappos' success lies in their focus on the company culture and delivering outstanding customer service. Twitter is one of the key tools that enables them to deliver an exceptional service. Practically every employee has a personal Zappos Twitter account and their tweets deliver interesting facts, helpful tips, the latest competitions, as well as personalised, one-to-one contact with consumers to help them through the buying process. All the employees come across as incredibly helpful and funny and the tone of their tweets feels like a conversation with a friend, not an online store. Direct access to Tony Hsieh, the hugely charismatic CEO is actively encouraged and at the time of writing he has over two million followers on his @zappos account, but he seems, no longer, to be tweeting.

Key Learning: Social media is part of the culture of Zappos and it is a very personal experience. No single person manages Twitter; instead helpful, funny tweets are sent by everyone from top management to the shop floor staff, all with the same positive, upbeat, friendly tone of voice.

DELL

Dell has had a social media renaissance. Today, there are multiple ways to connect with Dell online; numerous Twitter handles for niche customer communities and interests all over the world and over 100 employees use Twitter to connect with customers. They also have a network of blogs, YouTube channels and active Facebook pages. Dell lets people connect with them in the way that's meaningful to them. Twitter is particularly successful for Dell; it's both a customer service and sales outlet. They use Twitter to get instant feedback on products and services, to share information and to build relationships with customers, partners and influencers. They have generated seven figures in revenue through Twitter by messaging their followers when discounted products are available at the company's Dell Outlet Store. Recipients can easily click to purchase the product or forward it to others.

In 2007, Dell launched Idea Storm, a crowdsourcing initiative that encouraged people to submit ideas for Dell's products and services. It has received over 16,000[11] ideas and implemented close to 500, at ten a month, which is pretty impressive. As an overt demonstration of just how much they listen and value their customers, it has gone down very well.

Key Learning: Creating a community is central to Dell's strategy and listening to what this community has to say is a great way to identify gaps and find better ways of meeting customers' expectations. Dell uses social media as a way to build better relationships with customers, partners and influencers, which in turn leads to stronger sales.

11   Source: http://mashable.com/2011/08/25/dell-brand-suggestion-box/

OLD SPICE

In early 2010, Old Spice exploded over the Internet with a video campaign that went viral. It featured hundreds of personalised YouTube videos that responded by name to bloggers and fans who tweeted comments about the campaign. The campaign launched with "the man your man could smell like" video, featuring the "most interesting man in the world 2.0 Isaiah Mustafa". This was followed by a second video and they were seeded across social networks where viewers were encouraged to ask him questions. All the responses were tracked and users who contributed interesting questions or were high-profile people on social networks were responded to directly and by name through short, funny YouTube videos. They made close to 200 different videos including a response to Digg founder Kevin Rose, TV star Alyssa Milano as well as many others, famous and not.

You can view the campaign here: www.JacquelineBiggs.com/OldSpice

At the time of writing, the YouTube channel for this campaign has almost 300 million views! Testimony to how much people were enjoying the campaign, an Old Spice voicemail message for your phone was also created, not by the company, but by a crowd of users from Reddit, the social news site.

Key Learning: You will never create a viral video - only your viewers can. Finding new ways to engage and entertain your audience can result in extraordinary results. What worked really well was how the campaign appealed to peoples' egos and although not specific to individuals, felt incredibly personalised. The speed of the video creations was also central to the success of this campaign as it was very surprising to receive a personalised video shortly after asking a question. Anyone who received a video, plus a huge number who didn't then tweeted, Facebooked and shared the videos across their social networks. It was an explosive success.

BLOGS, EMAILS AND SECRET WEAPONS

To blog or not to blog

> "The bottom line is that blogging is like sex. You can't fake it. You can't fake passion. You can't fake wanting to engage with the public. If you do, it will ultimately be an unsatisfying experience for both the blogger and their readers."
>
> **Kevin Anderson**

Let's be clear - you don't have to start a blog. Many people can't think of anything they would rather do less, as the mere thought of writing a blog post breaks them out in a cold sweat. It can be a big undertaking and once you start, you need to stay committed. There's nothing worse than landing on a blog that hasn't been updated for months.

That said, there are a lot of advantages to having a blog, but, as with all social media activity, you have to be clear about your objectives and they need to be measurable. How can a blog help you to achieve your mission? Do you want to help people? Reach a new audience? Establish yourself as an expert? Collaborate with your customers on new product ideas? How will your blog contribute to achieving your broader business goals? If starting a blog is right for your business, you have to be clear about your objectives, as this makes it much easier to create a content strategy, as blogging with purpose gives you great focus.

GETTING STARTED

Ease yourself in gently. Start by finding blogs with a style, tone and content that you like and subscribe to them; they don't just have to be in your sector. Look at the content that gets the most comments and re-tweets and see if you can spot trends. Think about the role for your blog; do you want to entertain, to educate, to inform, to build a community, to establish thought leadership? Get clear about who you're writing for and why they will read your blog. Who do you want to attract? What are their goals, challenges and problems? What experiences can you share to help readers resolve problems? How can you connect what you offer, to your target readers and what they need and want?

WHICH PLATFORM?

There are numerous platforms available, I recommend Word-Press, as it's incredibly easy to use, but Blogger and Typepad are two more options to look at to decide your personal preference. If you don't have the skills to build the blog yourself, you can hire freelance developers relatively cheaply on sites like odesk. com, elance.com or guru.com. See the resource box below for more information.

GETTING SUBSCRIBERS

A lot of people like to read blogs in RSS readers (Really Simple Syndication) like Google or Netvibes, which put all the blogs and news sites you are signed up to in one place; such a timesaver! Other people prefer to subscribe to blogs by email, so make sure you give people both options. Sign up to FeedBurner to do this, as it creates the RSS feed and a "subscribe by email" box, and does all the techie stuff for you. RSS feeds are anonymous and don't require readers to part with any details in exchange for the feed, so you won't have the contact details for anyone that signs up to your feed.

WHAT TO BLOG ABOUT?

When deciding what to blog about, put yourself in the shoes of your target readers; how can the content that you create take your readers on a journey from where they are today, to where they want to be? Look at other blogs in your sector, as this will help you to see what's important and relevant to your audience and read industry press magazines to see which headlines draw you in. Take a look at Digg.com, a social news site where the top stories are measured by popular opinion across the web. People can vote stories up and down, called digging and burying, so search for stories in your sector and review the topics and headlines that do well.

You don't just have to write blog posts, you can create your own videos, or reference videos on YouTube, link to presentations in SlideShare, use photos, basically mix it up to keep it interesting, both for you and your readers. Flickr is a photo sharing website and you can use photos that have a "Creative Commons Licence" so long as you quote the source and link to the original, so it's always worth searching for visuals as this makes your blog more engaging for your readers.

It's worth creating a list of topics and if you can, create about ten blog posts before you launch your blog. That way you avoid writer's block and you buy yourself time to create new posts based on the success of your first ten. Plus you will then have more time to promote your blog and to write guest articles on other blogs to further extend your reach. Keep your content interesting and varied, a blog is not an ad or a press release, that would be way too boring! Your blog gives you a chance to humanise your brand and reveal your personality, even if your industry is quite serious, it doesn't mean you have to be.

The titles of your blog posts are extremely important, as your readers are bombarded with content day in, day out. If you want to get their attention, you need to write really good titles, but they need to contain keywords that are relevant to your target audience, so that your blogs appear in search results. Get inspiration from the front covers of leading magazines and model your titles on these, as the magazines spend a lot of money researching the headlines that sell. Make sure your layout is easy to read, if you're writing a long post, break it up visually with pictures and sub headings that make it easy to scan and dive in for those in a hurry.

ACTION

- ❑ How will a blog help you to achieve your wider business objectives? Define its role in your marketing mix.

- ❑ What type of blog do you want to create? Research the design, style and tone of voice that fits your brand.

- ❑ Create a profile of your ideal reader, who are they? Why would they read your blog? What type of content is relevant and useful to them?

- ❑ Decide whether you want to build your own blog or outsource it to a designer? Either way, be clear about what you want by reviewing other blogs.

- ❑ Create a list of ten blog posts that you want to launch with.

RESOURCES

If you don't want to build your blog site yourself, then brief it out to a designer. Be clear about what you want, perhaps choose your theme first, then write a brief outlining what you need and if you don't have a designer in mind, post it on one of the following outsourcing sites. Your brief will go out to freelance designers from around the world who will bid for your job. If you already have a list of blogs you like the design of, go to www.builtwith.com and enter the URL's to identify which content management system they are built with so you can then hire someone with the specific skills you want. Make sure you review their portfolio of work and contact their customers before hiring. Make sure you look at a designer's portfolio in detail and email two of their previous customers to check that they provided a good service. A key question to ask is how long it took to build, as in my experience, it always takes a lot longer than you think. If building your blog is time critical, then incentivise your outsourcer with bonus milestones, this usually speeds up the process!

- www.odesk.com
- www.elance.com
- www.guru.com

If you want to build it yourself, it's worth investing in a Word-Press theme, which is a very easy to use design template. I've used Thesis themes for some sites as there are some great tutorials to help you get started:

- www.diythemes.com

How to send your blog viral

> "If the Internet can be described as a
> giant human consciousness, then viral
> marketing is the illusion of free will."
> **George Pendle**

I hate to break it to you, but unless you are Paris Hilton, chances are, your content won't "go viral". Unfortunately, there is no blueprint for a successful viral campaign. However, there are steps you can take to increase the views of your blog posts and if your content is worth sharing, this can happen quickly.

BE SOCIAL

It helps to think of your blog as the central hub of your online communications, around which you create various outposts; Twitter, Facebook, Google+, YouTube channel, LinkedIn groups, forums, other people's blogs, Pinterest. The outposts that you choose will vary according to where your particular target audience likes to hang out. Each outpost has its own community and is therefore a great way to increase the reach of your blog and traffic back to your site.

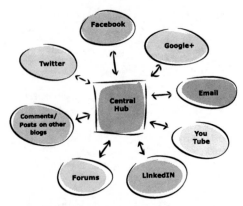

When you write a blog post, tweet about it, post it on your Facebook page, link to it from your LinkedIn page, "bookmark" it, "stumble it" and "digg it". In case all that left you thinking, "what the...." Let's go through each one and you can decide which are relevant for your target audience.

To share it on Facebook, Google+ and LinkedIn, create a new status update, write a couple of sentences to outline the content and add the link. Voilà. On Twitter write a tweet that is succinct, but intriguing to create interest. Use a URL shortening tool like bit.ly so that you don't use up all available characters with your url. Bit.ly also tracks the number of clicks, so is a good analytics tool.

> TIP: Research by Hubspot's Dan Zarella revealed that tweets that state "Please Re Tweet" get four times that number of re-tweets to those that don't ask. Interestingly, writing the whole phrase is important, as this is more effective than "Please RT". Try it for yourself and monitor the results.

Social bookmarking has been around for quite a few years now, instead of bookmarking pages in your browser to be viewed by you alone, they are stored on a social bookmarking platform and can be viewed by others if you want them to be. Social bookmarking not only puts your website in front of others who may not have discovered it but, in many cases those links count as a small vote in popularity when it comes to ranking your web page. The number of bookmarking sites has exploded over the years, but don't overload yourself, pick one or two and stick to them. Del.icio.us, StumbleUpon, Digg and Reddit are some of the main players to take a look at as they offer a great way to organise, store, manage and then search for your content later.

If you create videos for your blog then set up a YouTube channel for your brand and just link to the video in your post. If your videos are longer than fifteen minutes, you cannot post these on YouTube, so I recommend signing up to Vimeo which does not restrict the length of your video.

Pinterest can be a great source of traffic to your blog. You should create boards that relate to your blog topics and pin the images or videos from each blog, putting the URL of your blog post as the source.

Commenting on other blogs and forums in your niche is a great way to increase the visibility of your blog, as your sign-off includes a link to your site. However, never post for posting's sake, or just to link to your site, make sure that your comment adds genuine value to the discussion. It's your chance to show-case your thought leadership, so make it a valuable contribution. Your comments brand you and your business, so make them pique the interest of readers to want to hear more from you. You need to start by identifying relevant blogs in your niche, so use the sites detailed in the resource box to search. If it's a high traffic blog, you need to comment as soon as the post comes out for maximum exposure, as most people don't scroll down through all the comments. So subscribe to their blog and monitor when new posts go live and comment early. If you can, allocate thirty minutes a day to comments and you'll reap the rewards.

Once you have identified high traffic blogs in your sector, contact the owners and suggest possible topics that would be of interest to their readers and about which you could write a guest post. Always suggest multiple topics, so the blog owner has a choice. It goes without saying that they must be original posts.

CREATE MULTIPLE CONNECTIONS

Encourage your readers to connect with you on Facebook, Twitter, Google+, StumbleUpon etc. You can never have too many like-minded friends and as they share, re-tweet and like your content, their friends and followers will see it and some will connect with you too.

LOYALTY SCHEME

In the offline word, loyalty schemes are a great way to build a relationship with consumers and encourage repeat purchase. Whilst online equivalents exist, the smart entrepreneurs at Punch Tab have taken this one stage further and created a loyalty scheme around social sharing that rewards people for sharing content on a daily basis. It's a great way to build loyalty and awareness of your website or blog. So how does it work? When readers land on your site, a small pop up window alerts them that they can earn points for visiting and sharing your content if they sign up. Points mean prizes and you can set up a reward scheme to let readers win anything, from your products and services to Amazon vouchers, in exchange for liking and tweeting your content. In addition to the on-going loyalty programmes, you can also set up one-off giveaways to drive a fast response. Check them out as you can get started in minutes: www.punchtab.com

POST AT HIGH TRAFFIC TIMES

When you start out, experiment with posting blogs on different days and at different times. Then, when you have a high enough readership to identify trends, analyse your blog traffic and identify when posts get the most traffic and comments. Save your best posts for these times for maximum impact.

BE TOPICAL

If there's breaking news in your industry then write a post with your opinion on the turn of events. To stay up to date, subscribe to news feeds and the blogs of key players in your industry and respond quickly for greater visibility on Google.

ENCOURAGE COMMENTS ON YOUR POSTS

Asking your readers questions at the end of a post is a great way to invite comments. However, avoid generic questions such as "Why don't you tell me what you think?", instead, be really specific: "So do you think David Cameron should now step down?". If you want to get comments quickly then contact previous commenters and thank them for their last comment and invite them to respond to your latest blog. It's a great way to create a sense of community.

TIP: Do bear in mind the 1-9-90 rule. This was pioneered by Josh Bernoff and Charlene Li in their book *Groundswell*, and has quickly become a standard: 1% of your population will create content, 9% will comment or engage with it, and 90% will just browse. Keep this in mind when you're setting your KPI's.

MAKE SHARING EASY

Make it really easy for people to share your content online. Whilst there are various tools to help you do this, I recommend either Addthis.com or Wibiya.com as they both offer easy ways to add the key social sharing buttons to your blog or website. If you make it easy, your readers will share your content if they like it.

PAID ADS ON WEBSITES

Some blogs and websites accept advertising which can range from buttons, banners and text links on the site or within a newsletter to fully sponsored emails or section on their site. Look for an "Advertise" link on the site, or approach the owner directly. Review the site and decide on which section you want to be featured, as it's always better to be targeted, rather than "run of site" which means you could basically end up anywhere on the site.

BUYING ONLINE CLICKS VERSUS ONLINE IMPRESSIONS

When buying online ad space, e.g. banners and buttons, costs are usually based on volume of impressions or clicks. Impressions refer to the number of times your ad is seen on the site and these are usually priced on a cost per thousand (CPM - M is the Roman numeral for 1,000) basis. Alternatively, you can buy clicks, which is more cost effective, as you only pay for the number of people who click on your ad and go through to your site. If you buy on a CPM basis you pay according to the number of people who view the page on which your ad is featured, but might not actually have seen your ad as they were looking at other content. Whichever you decide to go for, enquire about their ad tracking technology; ideally they will use a third party system to validate clicks and impressions. Ask for case studies to identify if advertising on their site is actually effective. Before you go ahead with a deal, call up the advertisers that you see featured on the site and ask them how their campaigns are going. If traffic through to their site is low, review their offer and copy to make sure this is not the reason for low conversions. If you are considering running a promotion in a newsletter, then make sure that you sign-up for it first and contact the current advertisers to understand how effective it is for them.

ACTION

- ☐ If you already have a blog, analyse your previous posts; which topics got the most attention and created the most conversations?

- ☐ Are you using all the tools at your disposal to send your blogs viral? If not, take a look at those you don't yet use.

- ☐ Do you make it easy for your readers to share your posts on multiple sites? Review the two tools I suggested, Addthis. com and Wibya.com.

- ☐ Take a look at Punch Tab's loyalty programme and think about the incentives you could offer your readers in exchange for sharing your content.

RESOURCES

Guest blogs on high traffic sites in your niche are a great way to extend your reach and grow your subscriber base. Use the following sites to search for opportunities:

www.invesp.com/blog-rank

This ranking directory provides a lot of insight on different blogs in different niches; you can search by category using keywords.

MyBlogGuest.com

This is a forum community where bloggers give info about their blogs and then ask for guest posts from other users

Technorati.com

Look in the Top 100 blogs in the world or top 100 in your niche to which you can submit guest articles. Better still; look in the top ten blogs in your niche. Mostly, these are the blogs with lots of subscribers and authority. That's what you need.

Alexa.com

Look for top sites by country and by category, though not combined. You can also research a site's traffic and audience profile by entering the web address.

Alltop.com

AllTop is Guy Kawasaki's news aggregator site that covers a diverse range of niches and highlights the top sites and blogs in each.

Blogrolls on popular blogs in your niche

Often overlooked, this can be a great way to find blogs on which to guest post. Authority bloggers normally list other authority bloggers in their blogroll.

How to write your 'about me' page

> "Always be yourself, express yourself,
> have faith in yourself, do not go out and
> look for a successful personality and
> duplicate it."
> **Bruce Lee**

When creating a blog, it's important to spend time crafting your "About Me" page, as it will be one of the first pages new readers go to. An effective "About Me" page should cover the following:

Introduce you

Tell your readers who you are, what you do and why you have created this blog. Avoid using industry jargon, instead be human and write like you talk. Include a photo of yourself or your team so they can "meet" you; don't use stock photography, authenticity is key. Consider creating a video intro as it's a great way for people to meet the real and authentic you.

Build credibility

Why should people read your blog? What experience do you have that makes what you write credible. Do you speak and educate on your topic? Tell your story and don't be afraid to blow your own trumpet here. Keep it relevant; the number of GCSE's you've got and the name of your cat probably isn't relevant. If you have testimonials add them to this page; if possible include video testimonials, as these are incredibly powerful.

Build rapport

What problem or goal are your readers grappling with that makes what you write relevant and useful? Demonstrate that you understand their challenges and create empathy through this identification, as it's your chance to create a personal connection with your readers.

Make it easy to connect

Offer multiple ways to connect with you, so that readers can choose their preferred channel. You can create a sign-up form for people to send in questions or queries, but this feels far less personal than offering your email address and, or a phone number. Speed of response is critical, so make sure you share an email you check regularly.

ACTION

- ❏ If you already have a blog, look at how many views your "About Me" or equivalent page gets and, using Google Analytics, review how long people stay on that page.

- ❏ Tweak your content, so it covers the above four points and monitor the same stats two to four weeks later. Dwell time should increase.

Rules of engagement

> "Start with what is right rather than
> what is acceptable."
> **Kafka**

When creating a blog it helps to think about your rules of engagement; what's acceptable and what's not? Following are some guidelines that you can use as a starting point.

Keep it real

Be human and write in the first person as it's much easier to create a relationship.

It's not all about you

Comment on other people's blogs. If you have regular commenters who are also bloggers, take a look at what they write about and leave a comment or two. Commenting matters as much to them as it does to you. Consider adding a blog-roll of the blogs that you like.

Keep your blogging policy simple

If blogging contributions are company wide, it helps to put a policy and guidelines in place, but don't be too restrictive, as this will kill interest. A blogging policy should be similar to your email policy.

Be clear about your intentions

It is ok to sell in your blog posts. Just not every post. As a rule of thumb, combine content posts with sales posts on a 3:1 ratio in favour of content. If you include an affiliate link, be transparent, your readers won't mind if you tell them, but they will if you don't.

Don't delete the bad stuff

Moderate all comments before they go live to avoid spam and any undue negativity, however, don't delete negative feedback. You will rapidly lose credibility, as it's unrealistic to only have raving fans, no company does.

Make it easy to share

Make sure your blog and posts use all the social sharing tools available, so that people can easily share your content and extend your reach.

Create conversation

Ask specific questions in your blog about which you want people to comment. Be specific about exactly what you would like their opinion on, as this increases comments. You could also be deliberately controversial about something to spark debate.

Be consistent

The frequency of your posts is important, once a day might be too ambitious, so if it's weekly, stick to it, don't let it drop to fortnightly. Create consistency so your readers know what to expect. If you blog monthly bear in mind that it will take you a lot longer to drive up blog traffic than with more frequent posts.

Track your success

Use Google Analytics to track site activity; it's free and easy to set up goal tracking. If the objective of your blog is to drive sales, then monitor each promotion and identify the most effective. If your goal is customer engagement then track the number of comments, subscribers, views etc. Whatever your goal, it has to be measurable and tracked regularly. Take a look at Crazy Egg.

It's a useful tool that shows where people are clicking on your site; they offer a free month's trial and it's inexpensive to subscribe afterwards.

ACTION

❑ What are your rules of engagement for your blog? Tailor the above to suit you and your business.

❑ Do you regularly comment on key blogs in your niche? If not, identify two or three and set aside time each week to comment.

❑ Do you keep track of the effectiveness of your posts? Set up templates in excel to track key metrics and update and review each month.

❑ Once your blog gets regular traffic, take a look at Crazy Egg to understand where your readers are clicking on your site; ideally you want to have promotional content in the areas that are clicked the most.

Why email marketing rocks

> "Either write something worth reading or
> do something worth writing."
> **Benjamin Franklin**

A regular email can make your readers feel connected to you, particularly when it's personalised, but you need to get into the habit of creating emails that matter. Many companies just email their database with their latest blog posts, but this really is a missed opportunity. Email marketing can be incredibly effective, if (and this is a big if) you have a good relationship with your subscribers and you take the time to plan your content strategy.

Start by deciding on the role email marketing could play in your marketing mix. If you already have a blog, how do you want the two to interlink, what is the role for each? Do you intend your emails to be a key sales driver? Or are you trying to demonstrate your expertise? To where are you driving the traffic? Are you trying to create a greater sense of community? Maybe it's all of the above? Get clear on your objectives, as this will drive your content strategy. If you decide that email marketing will be a core sales channel, you need to carefully think about your strategy – if every email is a sales pitch your unsubscribe rate will be considerable.

THE BASICS

Sign-up to an email marketing software platform as this gives you access to a range of important statistics; number of sent mails, opening rates, click-throughs and number of unsubscribes. There are various options on the market and most offer a free month's trial to help you make up your mind. Check out the resources box for more information.

An effective way to build your database is to place a prominent sign-up box on the home page of your website or blog. To get people to part with their contact details, it helps to offer a juicy incentive that goes beyond just receiving your emails, but more on this shortly. The email marketing platform you choose provides all the technological "backend" of the sign-up form; they capture the contact details and enter them into a database. A sign-up box should be really simple, the less information you request, the more sign-ups you will get. You can always request more information at a later stage, but for now your objective is to build your database and the more information you ask for, the lower your conversions. When creating your form you can choose to make each entry field either mandatory or optional; I recommend making the following mandatory:

❑ First name (it is key to get their first name so that you can personalise correspondence later)

❑ Email address

❑ Qualifier – You may or may not need this, it depends on the nature of your business, but this could be product focused, demographic, geographic etc and should only be included if it dictates how or why you communicate.

If you really want to ask for additional details, make them optional at this stage.

As mentioned, to encourage people to sign-up you need to offer them a great incentive; what this is depends on the nature of your business, but it needs to be something of value to your audience. To make your life easy, make it downloadable or accessible online so that it can be automated; e.g. as soon as someone has signed up, they are sent an email with the link to download or view your incentive. This might sound complicated, but it is incredibly simple to set this up in your email marketing platform and there are video tutorials to help you. You could offer a digital free gift, such as a white paper, a training video or an article, I cover this in greater detail in the next chapter.

As soon as someone signs up, their contact details are immediately entered into an online database housed on your email marketing company's website. You simply log in to view the list and create and send emails when you're ready. If you already have email addresses of prospects and existing customers you should upload these to your email marketing platform and create separate lists for "existing customers" and "prospects", so that promotional content you send to each group can be tailored accordingly.

> TIP: Only upload contacts that have opted in to receive content from you. If they have not, then you need to send them an email, asking them to opt in to receive future emails from you. If you add them without their consent they can report you as a spammer and you risk being fined £5,000.

WELCOME EMAIL

Most people who sign up to receive your emails will be new to your site, so make them feel welcome. Create a fun and engaging welcome message that introduces you and lets them know the type of content you'll be sharing. Encourage interaction from this first point of contact; ask them to do something - respond to a question, post a tweet, watch a video, write a comment. You want to shift them from being passive readers to active. This sets a precedent that will make it easier to get them to buy from you later.

DAILY, WEEKLY, MONTHLY?

The frequency of your emails will be driven by your objectives, but don't over-commit yourself. Set a manageable frequency and stick to it. As you did for your blog, you might want to build a bank of emails before you launch, so that you have content ready to go and breathing space to create more. If you do, then you can set up auto-responder sequences with your email marketing software so that subscribers receive your emails on pre-determined dates, no matter when they sign up. This way you can deliver your best content in the best order and at the most effective frequency to every reader that finds you. Alternatively, you can send all subscribers the same "fresh" emails each week. Both are viable strategies and depend on your objectives.

YOUR EMAILS LIVE AND DIE BY THEIR SUBJECT LINE

Without a compelling promise that piques the interest of readers, the rest of your email is worthless. Well crafted subject lines are key to a successful email marketing campaign and it's worth spending time creating and testing them. Whenever you send out an email always split test your subject lines, this means creating two subject lines and sending them to an initial proportion of your database, the email with the highest number of opens has the most compelling subject line, so use this subject in the email to the remainder of your database. Ideally you want a minimum of 100 recipients in each segment to give you a robust indication of success. Most email marketing software has this functionality inbuilt, you just need to remember to use it, as your subject line is the first and potentially only impression you make on a prospective reader. Play around with personalising subject lines and monitor the opening rates; sometimes even the smallest change can have a dramatic effect, so test an exclamation mark versus a full stop and explore what happens if you just change one word. Whatever you decide to change, remember to only change one element at a time so that it's clear what is driving increased or decreased opening rates.

Subject line guidelines

❑ **Keep it short:** You don't have much room, so be as succinct as possible. Try and keep it under about fifty characters and remember to leave room for first name personalisation if you need to.

❑ **Be specific:** On reading your subject line there should be no doubt about what the content covers and it has to be interesting. Subjects with numbers in them tend to do well, so consider "5 Steps To..." or "7 Secrets to...." If relevant to your audience.

- ❑ **Write it last:** Craft your content first and allow this to inspire your subject line.

- ❑ **Get inspired:** Look at magazine and newspaper headlines for inspiration as they have spent a lot of money researching what sells, so see what jumps out at you and tweak it for your audience.

- ❑ **Test and evaluate:** Always, always, always split test the subject lines for every email you send out. Over time you will identify trends, so use the learnings to create killer subject lines.

CREATING CONTENT

Every email you send should be digestible, engaging and encourage your readers to take action. The layout of your email is as important as the content, as most readers scan emails quickly, only reading more if something catches their eye. With this in mind, embolden headlines and keywords in copy so that they stand out. Emails can be a great way to educate prospects about your products and services. You can address and overcome possible objections, build credibility and create trust and desire in what you have to offer. They are a great way to keep prospects engaged and reminded of your products and services until the time is right to buy. That said, it's not all about making a sale, you need to deliver content that is valued by your readers and focus on building a relationship. People need to know, like and trust you before they buy from you and creating engaging content is a great way to build a firm foundation. Depending on your niche, great content might range from practical tips and advice to video tutorials, to something that makes them laugh. The entertainment value of your content is important, as if you continually deliver high quality content your readers will keep opening your emails. Whatever the focus, include a clear call to action to train people to take action on reading your content, this could be a request to share your content, fill out a survey, watch a video as well as to take up a promotion. Make sure you do this in every email.

RESOURCES

- **Aweber:** www.aweber.com
- **MailChimp:** www.mailchimp.com
- **Marketer's Choice:** www.marketerschoice.com
- **Constant Contact:** www.constantcontact.com
- **Campaign Monitor:** www.campaignmonitor.com

Tips to avoid being unwittingly seen as spam

Many organisations use spam filters to auto-detect spam emails based on certain trigger characteristics, you need to know what the triggers are to avoid inadvertently including them. Whilst this is not an exhaustive list, knowing these can dramatically reduce the chance of your email going straight to the trash folder.

❑ Avoid excessive capitalisation and exclamation marks.

❑ Don't use the word Free in the subject line.

- [ ] Avoid spammy phrases such as "Click here", "Click below" "Once in a lifetime opportunity", "No risk", "Low risk", "No catch", "Money back guarantee".

- [ ] Don't use deceptive subjects to trick people into opening your email, pretending your email contains naked photos of Cheryl Cole, or a personal email from Richard Branson will only increase your unsubscribe rate.

- [ ] Don't pretend the email comes from a company or someone it doesn't. An email supposedly from Will.i.am is likely to have a higher opening than one from Bob Smith, but you will get reported as spam.

- [ ] Include a visible "Unsubscribe" button.

- [ ] Don't convert a Word file to HTML as this creates sloppy code.

- [ ] Don't create an email that is one large image file.

- [ ] Don't buy a list of contacts; build your own and clearly communicate what you will send out when they sign-up.

How to build a subscriber list

"Whatever good things we build,
end up building us."
Jim Rohn

Building and managing your database is a critical part of your business, as it is far easier (and more cost effective) to get existing customers to buy from you again, than it is to find new customers. Ideally you want to build a responsive list of customers that want what you sell long before you even tell them about it. Back in 2008, Kevin Kelly, a former Wired magazine editor, wrote a great post on his blog The Technium called *1,000 True Fans* and I encourage you to go and read it. He takes a look at the creative industries; artists, singers, writers, photographers and suggests that, instead of gunning for superstardom, they should focus on getting 1,000 true fans. A true fan, or as I refer to them, a raving fan, is someone that will buy almost anything you bring to market, love what you have to offer and tell all their friends about how great you are. He then gives the conservative example that if that fan spends a day's wages with you every year, say £100, and you had 999 others doing the same, you would earn almost £100k. That is far more than most artists, singers and writers are earning. It's also an incredibly realistic number, not least because of the explosion of social media. So, if you added one fan a day, it would take you three years. True fans do of course need nurturing, they want direct contact, they want you to keep in touch, they want a relationship with you, they want to know that you care. Today this is incredibly easy to deliver through social media channels.

Now, you might not be in the creative industries and you might need a whole lot more than £100k a year, but I'm giving you this example to get you thinking. How many true fans do you need? How much do they need to spend each year? Now, one of the strengths of the creative industries is that they tend to have low overheads but the same might not be true for you, this just means it might take you longer, but that's ok. Just get clear on your numbers and focus on building a community of raving fans.

ACTION

- ❑ What is the yearly net profit that you would like to generate in your business?

- ❑ In an earlier chapter you calculated your net profit per sale, use this figure to work out how many sales you need to generate to achieve your target yearly net profit.

- ❑ Calculate the frequency of purchase of your heaviest buyers over the course of a year. This is the closest you currently have to a raving fan.

- ❑ Now calculate how many raving fans you need to create to achieve your desired target.

- ❑ Once you get clear on your numbers, it makes the rest of the marketing puzzle a lot easier. Arguably your customer base will always be a mix of raving fans and the not-so-raving, but I just want to get you thinking.

HOW TO GENERATE SUBSCRIBERS ONLINE

In earlier chapters I outlined the importance of a prominent sign-up form on your blog or website and stressed how important it is to offer something of great value in exchange for someone's contact details. Depending on the nature of your business, this will vary. If you sell swimwear, offering browsers something entitled: "The ultimate bikini diet - how to shed 10 pounds in 10 days" with some impressive testimonials, might help to persuade them to part with their details. Whether you offer an e-book, a series of downloadable videos, a training course or a free sample is less important than the fact it has to be valued, free and preferably instant. It also has to be related to your brand, there would be little point offering "The guide to growing the perfect tomatoes" to someone in the market for cat food. Your giveaway is therefore a great way of pre-qualifying your list, as only those truly interested in your sector will sign-up. Change your giveaway each month and monitor the impact on the volume of subscribers.

TRACKING THE SUCCESS OF YOUR SIGN-UP FORM

You need to set up goal tracking in Google Analytics to track the effectiveness of different giveaways. As before, if you are not sure how to do this, just "ask" Google as there are numerous online tutorials. You want to monitor the percentage of people that see your page, sign-up and then download your giveaway.

HOW TO CREATE VALUABLE CONTENT FOR YOUR GIVEAWAY

Brainstorm giveaway ideas by thinking about the challenges and problems your target audience face, then think about what you could offer that could help to solve or alleviate them. It needs to be hugely compelling and a no-brainer. Just because it is free does not mean that you shouldn't invest time and money to create something of value. However, before you do, make sure it is actually going to be valued by your target, so ask them. Create a free online survey using Survey Monkey or Survey Gizmo and list out each option with a brief content outline and ask them to rate their interest on a five point scale:

1. Love it - give it to me right now!
2. Quite interested
3. I could take it or leave it
4. Not that interested
5. No way!

To drive response rates put a link to it on your home page, post the link across your social media sites and search for online forums relevant to your niche and post a link to your survey. Keep it short and don't limit it to just your suggestions, give respondents the opportunity to suggest something that they would like to receive from you, as this can be very insightful.

> TIP: To find an online forum in your niche, enter "name of your niche" followed by "forum" into Google.
> Review the content and make sure that it is currently active by looking at the dates of the last comments.

SIZE DOESN'T MATTER

Don't get hung up about the size of your subscriber list; it actually doesn't matter. What does, is how responsive and engaged it is, so focus on building a targeted database that regularly shares and comments on your content and buys what you offer. If twelve months ago you had a strategy in place that grew your list by just three people each day you would have gained over one thousand subscribers by now. So let's review a few strategies for growth.

HOW TO GROW YOUR LIST

Ask your readers to grow it for you

Asking your readers to share your emails with one or two people that they think will benefit from your content is a great way to grow your list. Don't pressure them, just ask, place the thought in their mind and you will find that they are willing to share.

Encourage existing customers to sign-up

Email marketing is a great way to cross-sell products and services to existing customers. They have already bought from you and you have heard me repeatedly say how much easier it is to sell a second product to an existing customer than the first one to a new customer. You should therefore devise a strategy to bring them into your email marketing funnel and there are various ways to do this:

- ❏ Add an opt-in form to the payment page.

- ❏ Promote your newsletter in any correspondence you send to them, such as email confirmations of purchase, delivery updates and beyond.

- ❏ If you only have their delivery address, then include a flyer in their next package that details the benefits of signing-up.

- ❏ Track and evaluate the uptake of each, so that you continually optimise your marketing activity.

Only share your best content on social media

Most people share all of their content across all social media channels, but it's natural that some of your content is stronger than others, so why not just share your best bits? Every month you could pick one or two posts or articles to share and this way you condition your connections to always expect great content from you, which results in an increase in re-posts and re-tweets. Ensure that at the end of the content to which you link, there is an opportunity to sign-up to receive your emails on a regular basis.

Have multiple ways to sign-up to your emails

The sign-up form on the home page of your website or blog will be a key driver of subscriber growth, but why not create more than one opportunity? Encourage sign-ups in every correspondence you send to your customers from email confirmations of purchase to delivery updates and beyond.

You could also test and explore other sign-up mechanisms that sit on your home page such as Viper Bar if your site is built on WordPress. It is a free downloadable plug-in that integrates with Aweber, MailChimp and FeedBurner; you can customise the message and design and it sits at the top of your site. Test different messages, run one for a month and a different one the next and monitor the results. One drawback is that you only get someone's email address and not their first name, so you can't send personalised emails later.

Wibiya is another useful tool. It is a customisable social toolbar that sits at the bottom of the screen and enables users to like the page, tweet content, post to LinkedIn and more. However sign-ups are limited to RSS feeds, but it's always useful to give people multiple ways to sign-up. It is also a great way to increase social media interactions on your site, as it sits on every page.

You can see it live here: www.brand-camp.com

Run a social promotion

Competitions can be a great way to grow your list and various online applications make it really easy to run them across social media where you can quickly reach a large, targeted audience. I'm a big fan of the Wildfire App that enables you to create branded sweepstakes, competitions, group buying deals and coupons in exchange for a small subscription fee. When offering prizes make sure that they build on your brand and act as a qualifier rather than have universal appeal, as you need to ensure you build a targeted database, not just a large one.

Set up a referral programme

Leverage the power of word of mouth and the connections of your existing customers and other relevant contacts through a referral programme. When incentivised this works well, but depending on the relationship with your list, it can be just as effective with no incentive at all. Make sure you test and trial both. If you have an online store, then Referral Candy offer an easy to use referral programme, once someone buys from your store they are emailed information about the referral programme and they can forward the email, or share discount codes with friends and family and if they buy, the referrer gets rewarded and you get a new customer. This can be effective at driving sign-ups if you add an email opt-in to the payment page.

Write guest blogs

I've already mentioned the value of writing guest blogs to drive traffic back to your site and with a highly visible sign-up form on your home page you are likely to convert some readers. An effective additional strategy is to link to some of the best content on your website within your post and position an opt-in form at the bottom. Engaged readers will click on your references and sign-up if they enjoy what they read.

Once you have researched and identified relevant blogs contact the owner and suggest a series of ideas for articles that their audience will love. Make your summary short and outline your central argument. Send them examples of your writing style so that they know you are not wasting their time. If you feel you already have a great article or video that's ideal for their audience, then send this as well and share some stats that justify why they should include it, e.g. it has a high number of shares, comments, views etc. If you intend to promote a product within your content, offer referral commission to your partner for any referrals that come from their site.

Create joint ventures

Joint ventures can be a very quick way to explode your list. First you need to identify the influencers in your niche; those with a big following who target the same audience as you. Typically they have a high traffic blog or website with lots of repeat traffic and a highly connected audience. When reviewing their sites, look at how many comments each post or article gets, which will give you a good indication of their relationship with their readers. Spend time reading their articles, note the style and layout of their posts and identify the type of articles that get the most comments.

Even though your objective is to get the influencer to promote your brand, it's a two way street, so think about what you could offer that would be of interest first. You could start by offering to promote their products or services to your database, you could offer to interview them to promote them and share the interview with your list. Perhaps one of their articles influenced your business; send an email and a thank you, so you get on their radar, as this is more effective than a completely cold email.

Comment on forums and blogs in your niche

I've previously outlined how posting valuable tips, advice and comments on blogs and forums in your niche can be a great source of traffic to your site. It can also be an effective way to increase subscribers, particularly if you have a devoted landing page for your sign-ups as you can add the direct URL to your signature. It's less effective when your sign-up is part of your home page, as there are more distractions on the page. That said, there is no reason why you can't create a bespoke landing page as well. I cover how to do this in the next chapter.

Following any one of these strategies will help you to grow your database, quickly and effectively. I recommend that you test each one and learn what works in your niche.

ACTION

- ❑ Brainstorm a series of ideas for giveaways and create an online survey to identify the most appealing to your target.

- ❑ Set up goal tracking on Google Analytics to monitor the effectiveness of different giveaways.

- ❑ Do you have multiple ways to sign-up to your blog and emails? Do you include a sign-up option on your checkout page? At the bottom of your blog posts? Review Wibya and Viper bar and test them on your site.

- ❑ Take a look at Referral Candy's programme, could your company benefit from it?

- ❑ Outline a subscriber growth strategy that you want to run next month and plan a schedule of tests for the next six months.

How to create effective sign-up pages

> "We are all experts in our own little niches."
> **Alex Trebek**

The most effective way to drive sign-ups to a promotion or to your email list is to create a bespoke landing page, that single-mindedly focuses on this objective. Be warned, it might not be the most beautifully designed page you have every created, but if you follow some layout guidelines, it could be one of the most effective.

I have spent a lot of time researching and monitoring landing pages with high conversion rates and it's shown me that there are a few key ingredients that can have a dramatic effect. What I love most about Internet marketing is that it's so easy to build a page, track activity and optimise it. I can give you a great starting point based on tried and tested effective layouts and I challenge you to blow the doors off the conversion rates by optimising it for your niche. I only ask that you then email me to brag about it. My contact details are at the end of the book.

5 STEPS TO AN EFFECTIVE SIGN-UP PAGE

1. Know your niche

Step into the shoes of your target audience and think about what makes your products and services relevant and desirable. What problems do they help your targets to solve? How will they make your audience feel when they receive them? How will your products or services impact on their life? What could happen if they didn't have them? How you answer these questions will help to shape how your present and position your products or services. The more specific you can be the better, as you need to build a qualified list.

2. What do you want them to do?

When creating an opt-in landing page the sole focus is to get them to sign-up. This objective drives every element on the page and if it doesn't, discard it. You don't want to clutter the page with links to social media outposts or any other distractions, if you want this page to be effective, you have to be single-minded. One page. One action.

3. The key ingredients

There are five key ingredients to any successful landing page:

1. Sign-up form
2. Killer headline
3. Motivating benefits
4. Clear call to action
5. Social proof

❏ **Sign-up form:** The objective of your page is to build your database and create a list of subscribers to your emails. So before you get started, decide on which email marketing company you want to use to provide the "backend". Once you have created the form, make sure that you test the mechanic when it's live on your site. The sign-up form should sit above the fold and be very prominent on the page.

❏ **Killer headline:** This is the key hook that will keep people on your page, so you need to instantly grab their attention. Your headline should draw them in and make them want to hear what you have to say. Avoid being misleading or too generic, be clear about what you're offering.

❏ **Motivating benefits:** What is the key reason that people will sign-up? Go back to step one and review your responses. What are you offering them and how will it benefit them? Be clear and concise, don't try and be clever with your copy. If you're offering free gifts in exchange for their details, tell them what they are and why they're valuable. Always test and research your giveaways to make sure that they are desired by your target market and not just what you think they need.

- ❑ **Clear call to action:** Make it really obvious what you want someone to do. Use arrows to highlight where they need to put their details. If you create a video then tell them what you want them to do, as well as point them to where they need to sign-up. As mentioned, there must be only one call to action, don't dilute the effectiveness of this page by having multiple clickable elements.

- ❑ **Social poof:** Testimonials are a great way to build your credibility and increase sign-ups. What do your existing subscribers think of your emails, your free gifts and products and services? Simply ask them if they have not already volunteered this information. Never make up your testimonials, as if this is uncovered, your credibility will plummet. If you already have subscribers, then add a tally indicating the number so far, as many people won't want to miss out.

4. Test and evaluate

How you layout the page can have a dramatic effect on the success of your page. Despite my tips, you still need to test everything. Where should the sign-up box sit, on the left or the right? Is your headline helping or hindering? Do you need to write more copy? The only way to answer this is to test, test, test. Create a split test, this is two landing pages that are exactly the same bar one element and monitor effectiveness. Play around with all of the elements on the page, one after the other. Create different gifts, change the size and colours of fonts, as well as the number of arrows, the size of the video, the box etc. This is key to creating an effective page. It is critical to only change one element at one time, otherwise you cannot be sure what is driving the change. There are a number of elements to play with so take your time and track the sign-up conversion rate after each change, but make sure that each test has a robust number of views before you make decisions. Ideally around 1,000 impressions is robust enough, but if you are targeting a very small niche, then this will need to be smaller, so use your judgement, but try not to go under 100.

5. Video versus copy

I am not a fan of the incredibly long, scrolling sales pages, littered with "Buy Now" buttons. In my experience, video is much more effective, so I strongly recommend creating a video as opposed to pure copy on your landing page; it's much more engaging. If you like being in front of a camera it's also a great way for potential customers and clients to meet the person or people behind your brand. If the mere idea of seeing yourself in a video is too much to handle, you can always just have your voice and a series of images, or get someone else to present for you. Your video should create a strong, motivating case to take the desired action. Make the most important points at the start of the video to hook your listeners in. Be persuasive, but avoid any hard selling.

Creating a video does not have to be an expensive undertaking, it can even be something you create yourself using a web ready video camera for easy upload. See the resource box for tools to help you do this. However, if budgets allow, then a professional video can be very effective as they are skilled in creating engaging content. Remember that some people will prefer to read copy than watch a video, so include the key points from the video as copy on the site, but make sure you give them a reason to watch the video, as it will help your conversions. Note that in my experience, sites that convert really well have a sign-up box on the right hand side of the page and a video on the left.

Following these five simple steps will help you to create an effective landing page.

RESOURCES

Web ready cameras

(If you can stretch to HD, then this improves the quality of your videos)

- Kodak Play series
- Kodak Zi8
- Flip cam

Tripod

- Joby Gorillapod
- Lupo Mini Portable Tripod stand

Microphone

- Audio Technica ATR 3350 - good when starting out
- Snowball Microphone (for Mac users)
- Yeti Microphone (for Mac users)

Screen recorders

- Screenflow (Mac)
- Screenium
- Jing (5 minutes free or paid option)
- Camtasia (PC)

How to influence the influencers

> "Advertising reflects the mores of society,
> but it does not influence them."
> **David Ogilvy**

Relationships between people have always been invisible, but social media has made the invisible visible and so controllable. With a few clicks of a button we can now identify the most connected people in our network and our industry. It seems logical that your marketing could be more effective if you influenced the people that your target look up to and by whom they are influenced. But how do you go about this?

WHAT DOES IT MEAN TO BE INFLUENTIAL?

Influence is made up of three components - not one of these relates to the size of a network. Influence is not a popularity contest, it's about inspiring others to take action.

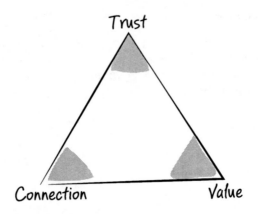

Trust: Trust is the cornerstone of influence, without trust it is impossible to influence.

Value: To have an impact you need to deliver value and be seen as an authority.

Connection: There needs to be a bond, a genuine and meaningful connection between the influencer and the influenced.

When these three components collide, true influence can take place. These are important traits to look for in the relationships that influencers have with their tribes, but they are also traits that businesses need to develop if they want to influence their own network. It's critical to identify and define what value means to your audience, as only then can you ensure that you deliver.

TOOLS TO HELP YOU FIND SUPER CONNECTED INFLUENCERS

There are various tools available to help you identify the online movers and shakers in your sector. However, to make things complicated, each tool has a different way of calculating influence. This does call into question the validity of each of their supposed influencers, particularly when the results between tools are not always consistent. Setting the purity of the data aside for a moment, the tools do at least give you a good starting point for investigation.

Here are some of the key rating companies:

❑ **Klout** - they assign a Klout score based on the number of people you influence, your level of influence and then the influence of your network.

❑ **Peer Index** - they assign a PI score by reviewing your authority, so how much people rely on your opinions, the level of engagement with your audience and your level of activity.

❑ **Kred** - These guys measure influence and outreach. Here your influence score is a measure of your ability to inspire others. It is a number on a scale from 1 to 1,000, and is based on how often your tweets are re-tweeted, how many new followers you gain, and how many replies you generate. Kred does take into account Facebook likes and Google +1s, but Twitter is the main source of data. It is a lot like your Klout score. The Outreach score is measured in levels and is a reflection of how generous you are with re-tweeting and replying to others. Calculating your Kred score is free, but they also offer paid social media monitoring solutions.

- ❏ **Socmetrics** - These guys identify influencers based on specific topics taking into account peer validation and topicality, i.e. whether you interact with other influencers on your topics and if so, do they re-tweet, share and so on, plus how much your content is on topic and your ability to drive action. They consider multiple channels and reach including YouTube, Twitter and blog readership.

- ❏ **Technorati** - These guys publish the top 100 blogs based on the "Technorati Authority" score, they cover a number of sectors, but not all.

In summary, the first three are largely skewed by Twitter activity and Technorati is solely focused on blogging, whilst Socmetrics, the relatively new kid on the block, seem to be the most well rounded; it is a paid service, but worthwhile.

HOW SHOULD YOU CONNECT WITH INFLUENCERS?

Once you have identified the most influential people in your niche start to build a more in depth profile of each influencer. Take a look at the type of content they share, what do they re-tweet and post to their network? Do they share articles, deals and discounts, research, videos, games, contests? Divide up your influencers into different groups; one of my clients divides her influencers into "Discount Divas" - who love to share the latest deals, "Experts" who pass on the latest research, how to articles, Top 10 lists etc, "Gaming Geeks" who share competitions and games, and "Entertainers" who share YouTube videos, movie trailers etc. Once you identify the type of content they like to share, you can tailor what you create and find smart ways to connect with them, so that they pass it on.

Make them famous

We all like to feel special and know that what we do makes a difference. Getting attention and recognition is hugely motivating, even when you are a key influencer, I've run several campaigns that have demonstrated this. For one of my clients we offered exclusive content to the top sharers. The campaign was effective but it really took off when we added an online scoreboard of the top sharers to the home page of the website. As the results were so visible, competitive natures kicked-in and unique visitors from shared links more than doubled. They were all vying for the top spot. Simple, but very effective.

Bring it offline

Some of the most successful influencer programmes that I have run involved meeting the influencers in the offline world. We created an exclusive event for a client that twenty influential bloggers were specially selected to attend. We gave them gifts, pampered them for a day, but also got to ask their opinion on the latest new product development ideas. We got incredible research insights and they felt trusted and valued and also had a great day out. They also loved meeting the other bloggers, as whilst they all knew each other online, they had never met face to face. Following this event, we had a LOT of incredibly positive reviews and posts that lasted for months.

Give and you shall receive

Reciprocity is the not so secret ingredient to a successful social media campaign. If you want your influencers to share your content and talk positively about your brand, what can you give in return? What's of great value to them? Direct access to you or the top executives in your company? A night on the town? Exclusive content? Being the first to receive new products? Being invited to take part in research? If you're not sure, you can always just ask them what they would most like to receive.

Guest posts

If your influencers have their own blogs, then writing a guest post on their blog can be a great way to increase your brand awareness and drive traffic to your site. Don't just launch straight in and ask to write a guest post, remember you want to create a relationship first. Read their blog and understand their tone of voice, the type of content that works for their readers, comment, share their content, spend some time doing this so that they notice you. After a few weeks, be proactive and suggest an irresistible blog post that their readers will love. It has to be original and ideally spark a debate. If you do this well, a guest post can be a great source of new business leads if you drive them to a sign-up page on your site. Do make sure your site can handle the extra traffic though.

Don't forget you're human

Whilst connecting across social media platforms is useful, the strongest relationships are still built in the real world. With the world at our finger tips, it's so easy to forget the human touch. We're all busy and it's far easier to send an email, or re-tweet a post than it is to find time to have a coffee with someone. You need to re-think this. A coffee with a journalist that regularly reports on your sector is going to have a far greater impact than an email out of the blue asking for something. The same goes for influential bloggers; they are clearly online addicts, but sometimes the offline world is just as interesting to them.

The trick is to find out where they go. I am not suggesting you stalk them, but you do need to get up close and personal. For example, if you're a tech start-up, you will find most of your influencers at SXSWi's yearly event (South by South West Interactive) in the USA, so go there and meet them in person. Alternatively, if you identify an influential blogger, read their historical posts; what events has he or she been to in the past? Chances are they will go again. Be a detective. When you do track them down, the idea is not to sell to them, it's to make friends, just go and hang out, buy them a coffee or a beer and find out what they're up to. We all want to do business with friends, not pushy sales folk. When the time comes, of course you talk about your business, but it's not a conversation starter. For this approach to be effective you need to identify locations where you can meet a number of influencers at once, do your research, it's easier than you might think.

ACTION

- ❑ Review each of the rating tools and search for influencers in your sector. Note similarities between the tools.

- ❑ Decide on the top five influencers you want to connect with over the next month. Sign-up to their blog, follow them across social media and connect, comment and share their content so that you get on their radar.

- ❑ At the end of the month, if they are local, suggest meeting up, or if they are attending an event, go along and introduce yourself. Avoid the sales chat and focus on what they are up to and how you might be able to help them.

RESOURCES

In addition to the above influence measurement tools, there are a number of useful tools to help you to track the reach of your influencers. I find it's useful to create a spreadsheet and for each influencer I track key metrics such as site traffic, unique users, subscribers, and most influential topics. I then monitor changes every quarter.

- **Quantcast** - Measures site traffic and audience characteristics so you can identify what your target audience are viewing. Also suggests other sites your audience go to. Very useful. www.quantcast.com

- **Compete.com** - Ranks and profiles sites, similar to Quantcast, though to get audience data you need to pay. www.compete.com

- **Alexa** - Measures traffic, demographics, identifies hot topics and hot products and lots more: www.alexa.com

- **Vidstatsx** - Tracks YouTube influencers and enables you to identify the most influential YouTube channels; who has the most subscribers, most viewings etc. www.vidstatsx.com

- **YouTube Subscribers** - YouTube have their own stats - here you can identify most discussed videos, most viewed in your niche etc. www.youtube.com/charts

STRATEGIES FOR GROWTH

The only three ways to grow your business

> "I don't look to jump over seven-foot bars,
> I look for one-foot bars I can step over."
> **Warren Buffet**

Whether you are in the business to business market or business to consumer, if you want to grow your business there are only three ways to do it. That's it. There are just three critical metrics that you need to focus on improving and the adoption of a few simple strategies can help you do just that.

So, here are the only three strategies for growth in business:

1. Increasing penetration (volume of customers/clients).
2. Increasing frequency of purchase.
3. Increase average spend.

So let's take a look at each of these critical metrics:

1. NUMBER OF CUSTOMERS / CLIENTS

It goes without saying that this metric needs to go up over the course of a year, but what you also need to track is by how much it is growing (or declining) each month and then identify what's driving these rates. You need to be really analytical and review each sales and marketing channel so that you can track their effectiveness at growing your customer base. This way you can do more of the good, effective stuff and less of the not so effective. Without this insight you will keep doing both. You need to be able to segment your customer base into profitable niches, which might be by location, by customer type or motivation for purchase, by age, by sex or whatever makes sense for your business. Then, for each segment, you need to drill down to the monthly rate of growth or decline and identify what is driving the results.

ACTION

- ❏ Calculate your total number of customers.
- ❏ What is the best way to segment your customer base? Review the "Characteristics of profitable niches" box which can be found in the earlier chapter, "How to avoid marketing suicide".
- ❏ Review the rate of growth month on month over the last year for each segment and the total customer base, look for seasonal trends and calculate an average rate of growth. This is your benchmark.
- ❏ If you can't profile your customer base in a meaningful way, you need to address this immediately. List out the information you need to know for each customer and find a creative way to incentivise them to share it with you.

2. FREQUENCY OF PURCHASE

What is the average buying cycle for your business? How frequently do your customers or clients buy from you? How does this differ by product or service and by segment? Profile your heavy, medium and light buyers, how large is each segment? What are the key characteristics that make their buying behaviour different? Identify the frequency of purchase for each segment and monitor how this changes over time so you can identify trends in buying behaviour.

ACTION

- ❏ Calculate how often your customers buy from you - whether this is per year / month / week depends on the nature of your business.
- ❏ Again, do this by segment and identify trends.
- ❏ If this data is not available, put steps in place to set this tracking up.

3. AVERAGE SPEND PER TRANSACTION

On average, how much do your customers spend at each transaction? Analyse this at a total customer level and then by each segment. What trends can you identify now? What customer groups spend more each month and why? What promotions or packages could you put in place to encourage higher spend?

> **ACTION**
>
> ❑ Calculate the average value of a transaction at a total customer level and then by segment as relevant.
>
> ❑ If this data is not available, put steps in place to set this tracking up.

INSIGHT INTO ACTION

Remember the "10% strategy" I introduced you to at the start of this book? I demonstrated that if you increase the volume of leads, the conversion rate, the average spend and the frequency of purchase by just 10%, this has a dramatic effect on turnover. This strategy is even more effective when you apply it to your most profitable customer segments. For example, it would be much more profitable for you to focus your marketing on encouraging your heavy buyers to spend 10% more on each purchase and to buy 10% more times per year than it would be to offer the same promotions to your light buyers. If you segment your customer base you can be incredibly targeted with your promotions, minimising wastage and maximising returns.

Getting under the skin of these three metrics provides important insights into how and why your customers are buying your products and services. You can then laser focus your marketing to maximise your budgets. These kind of analytics are how blue-chip companies devise their marketing strategies, the insights *always* come from data. That said, not all the multinationals get it right though, as some are not collecting accurate data on their customers, which is incredibly wasteful. I used to be a frequent buyer of Tropicana orange juice; week in, week out I would buy at least one carton of orange. One day, I received discount vouchers through my door, offering me seventy-five pence off my next two purchases of Tropicana and yes, it included the one I bought religiously. What a waste. Surely the objective of their promotion should be to bring new consumers to their brand, or at least encourage me to try a different flavour. They clearly didn't collect accurate consumer data, which for a big brand like Tropicana is a big and very costly mistake. It's possible that this promotion had a high uptake, but when you consider that they were rewarding people who bought their brand anyway, you start to question the real value.

In contrast, Boots is a fantastic example of a company that uses their consumer data in a very smart way. The Boots Advantage loyalty card enables them to get a rich and detailed picture of exactly what their customers buy. Every quarter they send out targeted promotions reminding customers how many points they have and encouraging them to go in store via relevant and highly targeted promotions.

Tesco is of course the king of data mining. The Tesco Clubcard is presented to consumers as a great way of getting discount points that can be exchanged for discount vouchers or air miles. For Tesco, it is a great way to understand shopping habits and key trends in consumer buying behaviour as they have access to 13 million households. Dunnhumby, a data analysis company now owned by Tesco, analyses all the data looking at shopping trends at a postcode level and sells it on to other retailers to enable them to deliver tailored promotions to Tesco's customers. Dunnhumby made profits of £53 million in 2010. Furthermore, Tesco is said to have saved £350 million a year thanks to the Clubcard data, as it tailors its stock to meet demand, stocking only those products in local stores that sell in vast quantities. For some, it all feels a bit Big Brother, but from a business point of view to be able to tailor stock with postcode accuracy is revolutionary.

So, as you analyse your data, identify trends and opportunities between the segments and review the next chapter's strategies for ideas on how you can then turn these insights into action through targeted communications. I recommend spending at least six months to a year testing, evaluating and optimising different strategies to improve each metric. It helps to put six monthly objectives in place with monthly targets to keep you focused, then at the end of every month evaluate the impact of your activity and focus on how you could improve it. If you take a backward step one month, so be it, the importance here is to learn what works and what doesn't. Focus on failing faster and you will be successful more quickly. When you start out, treat you marketing campaigns as if they are always in beta. The more you test, evaluate and optimise your marketing the more effective it will become. I cannot stress this enough. Different markets have different nuances and whilst there are guiding marketing principles that I can teach, you need to fine tune your marketing strategy for your niche market and business.

Customer acquisition strategies

> "I can't give you the formula for success,
> but I can give you the formula for failure:
> Try to please everybody all the time."
> **Bill Cosby**

Once you are clear on your objectives for growth, you need to consider your strategy for achieving your goal. If you want to grow your customer base, consider the following strategies.

INCREASE AWARENESS

Growing your customer base is critical to any start up and small company. Many entrepreneurs believe that one of the key factors hampering their growth is that their target audience just doesn't know that they exist and if they just had bigger budgets they could advertise more and build greater awareness, faster. I'm afraid that's just not true, it's simply an excuse. Success is not determined by the size of an advertising budget, but by smart, creative strategies.

There is a tendency to believe that if you're relatively unknown, it is pretty hard to get featured in mainstream media, by mainstream I mean on TV, radio and in national papers. However, I was once given the greatest insight from a top journalist; newsrooms are often desperate for stories as the news channels are on 24 hours a day, which is a lot of airspace to fill. If you can help to deliver something topical and relevant, then proactively suggest your angle to the newsroom. Chances are you'll get featured. Why? Because most people do not do this.

As with anything in life, if you take action, you get results. I'm not saying that you will be successful every time, but it does work. Challenge yourself to think of ways to get your brand featured, start by considering the following:

Be topical

What's in the news right now that you can piggy back? Scour the headlines each day and if there is a topical story that you can legitimately comment on, then call up the press offices and tell them. However, unless you are one of the only experts in the world on this subject, I wouldn't go straight to the national channels or papers. Start local....really local if you need to. Once you get one or two bits of coverage, you're on a roll. Particularly if you have managed to get onto a local TV station, as they then know that you are not a lunatic. Of course it is unlikely that you will get to the producer (TV) or editor (press) on the first call, but you have to be tenacious. Ask for their contact details, the best way to connect with them and the right time to call back. Then call back...repeatedly. Every ten minutes if you have to. You will get there.

Be controversial

Is there anything happening in your market sector that you can challenge? I'm not suggesting you be controversial for the sake of it, but are bigger competitors getting anything wrong that you get so right? See if you can find an opportunity to position yourself as a superior alternative and get on the phone to the newsroom and create a press release. Britain loves the underdog.

Be strategic

If you send a press release to a journalist telling them about your new line of baby clothes, it's unlikely that you will get featured. If you send your baby clothes to celebrities with children and they wear them, then journalists are much more likely to talk about your label. Find out the address of their agents and start there.

Be resourceful

There are a number of services that journalists use when they are looking for quotable experts for a story and most can be signed-up to for free. I have listed the three that I use in the resource box below. These are a phenomenal resource as active requests come straight into your in-box and you can quickly scour them for relevancy and reply to the lead.

There are a couple of tips to help you get quoted:

Be quick

The speed of your response is critical, if you can't turn it around within an hour or two, then your chance of being quoted rapidly diminishes.

Make it easy

Be clear and concise. Don't hint at your expertise in a way that requires them to call you for more information, they might not have time. Include a few headline style quotes that they can just copy and paste into the article if they have a tight deadline and add a longer, more in-depth response if you need to below. Don't forget to include your phone number and email so that they can contact you if they do need more information.

Big yourself up

Don't be afraid to blow your own trumpet, they are looking for experts and you need to position yourself as the most credible source they will find. It's also a good idea to adapt your business title to suit the request....

Track your quotes

Journalists are super busy and they don't always have time to tell you that you have been quoted, so make sure that you don't miss it! Set up online alerts on your name.

Leverage it

As your media coverage builds, add a page to your website to showcase your expert status and link to it when you respond to quote requests to build your credibility.

So, now you have no excuses for not getting your brand name out there. The above approaches don't cost money, but they do take time and tenacity. Be an opportunist and seize the moment.

INCREASE DISTRIBUTION

Expanding and extending where and how your products and services are distributed is a great way to acquire new customers. However, if you are just starting out, getting stocked by major distributors is no mean feat. They squeeze margins, hold all the power and their decision making process is extraordinarily long, as are the lead times to actually get your product on the shelf. So think laterally and explore other routes to market. Once you're more established you will then have better bargaining chips.

Consider the following:

Explode your growth through strategic alliances

Customer acquisition costs can be one of your biggest business costs and if you have a long repeat purchase cycle you can end-up cash-strapped pretty quickly. Strategic alliances with other businesses targeting the same niche provide a smart way to lower acquisition costs to as little as the cost of a call to the business owner.

Don't compete, complement

I've always subscribed to the "if you don't ask, you don't get" approach to life and when it comes to starting a joint venture, it's never been more true. Write a list of non competing businesses that perhaps offer a product or service that precedes or follows yours, or maybe that just simply targets the same niche as you. Shortlist those you are most interested in and think about how you want to structure the deal. Spend time considering what you could propose that would make it an absolute no brainer to accept your offer. Consider offering to pay for all associated marketing costs and, or post and packaging. Perhaps you want to create a unique offer for their clients, this could include special terms and conditions such as a longer refund period, or an extended warranty. When crafting your proposal, it helps to quote facts and figures that support your sales success to date, such as current conversions, monthly sales revenues, average order value, whether it's your best selling product and so on. Transparency is key and a critical building block in a joint venture, so never, ever inflate your costs or lie about your conversions. It also helps to forecast the potential sales revenues they could expect if they promoted your product for say, three to six months. The larger the number, the juicier the proposition. The objective is to build an enticing commercial opportunity to which it's hard to say no, as you're doing all the legwork.

If however, you are struggling to convince another company of the brilliance of your idea, then suggest you start by running a test campaign. If this delivers the volumes that you anticipate, then you roll it out. Once you have the partnerships in place, create case studies and get testimonials from your partners, as this will help you to grow your strategic alliances quickly.

> TIP: If cash flow is not a problem for your business,
> then you could also offer 100% of the profit on
> the first sale to a potential partner, you know you
> make money from future sales, so it's a great way
> to secure a deal.

Strategic alliances do of course work both ways, so when constructing a deal to sell another company's products to your customer base, if you know there's more money to be made in repeat sales, then you could ask for 0% commission on the first sale in exchange for a healthy amount of future sales. This can be a very motivating proposition to a business owner, as they get access to a targeted customer base with limited risk.

Once you have run a few joint venture deals with your own customer base, you can then calculate the new lifetime value of your customers. Not only do they buy your goods and services, but they also buy your partner's, so the profit you make per customer has increased. This means the amount available to spend on marketing and sales has increased. It's all about the numbers and once you understand them, you can unlock profit you didn't realise even existed!

Famous strategic alliances

❑ American Express & British Airways

❑ Disney & McDonald's

❑ Innocent & Starbucks

❑ H&M & Stella McCartney

White label joint ventures

The most straightforward joint venture model is to promote your existing products or services to a new audience, as outlined above. It's distribution focused and a fast way to test the strength of a new route to market and build brand awareness. An alternative, non brand building option, is to white label your product or service. This essentially means that you remove all reference to your brand and another company brands your product or service as their own. It can be incredibly lucrative and is in fact the sole business model for a number of successful software companies. Supermarket branded products are mostly white label products, also known as private label, which are usually the cheaper alternative to the branded goods on the shelves and often outsell their branded competitors. As the share of sales of supermarket branded products has increased, so as not to miss out on sales, some of the bigger manufacturers have started to create and supply their existing products to the supermarkets and they package them as their own. Kraft, Unilever, Heinz and Del Monte are just a few examples.

Trade shows

Research the options in your market and then request a list of the previous year's exhibitors and give similar sized companies a call to see how successful it was for them. Never listen to the marketing spiel of the sales guy, do your own research and select your own companies to call and ask them what return on their investment they generated. Be wary about signing-up to brand new trade shows, as success is down to the quality of the attendees and if the organisers have not run it before, they might struggle to drive the footfall.

Affiliate marketing

This is when you get other people to promote your products or services in exchange for a commission. It is a form of joint venture but it can be much more structured as, depending on your industry, you can work with an affiliate marketing network such as Commission Junction or Shareasale and leverage their existing bank of affiliates, or you can create your own affiliate programme – both for people in your industry and for your customers (see next option)

Refer a friend schemes

Leverage the connections of your existing customers; as contented buyers of your products and services they can be highly persuasive. If they love your brand, chances are their friends and family will too, so why not reward them for sharing the love. In today's frugal times, this can be very effective. As noted earlier, Referral Candy offer a ready made scheme with performance based commission.

BRAND EXTENSIONS

New product development is a longer term strategy, but an effective way to bring in new customers. Successful brand extensions build on your existing brand and complement your current brand portfolio. The most famous success stories are Virgin's move into trains, planes and space or Apple's extension into iPods, iPhones and iPads. However, a brand extension can be a very risky venture, as even the big brands don't always get it right. Anyone remember Virgin Jeans or Virgin vodka? Exactly. Successful extensions transfer the benefits of your brand to the new products or services, increasing trust and giving you greater certainty of success. If you're considering extending your brand, get clear on what you're known and loved for by your current consumers and think hard about how you can extend this into another category.

RE-POSITIONING

Re-positioning your products or services can broaden their appeal and bring in additional customers, but this is also a much longer term strategy. Kellogg's Special K launched the Special K challenge a few years ago, which encouraged people who wanted to lose weight to substitute two meals for bowls of Special K in order to lose around six pounds in two weeks. Suddenly Special K was seen as more than just a breakfast cereal, it could help you to drop a dress size, so the brand became more appealing to brides-to-be, new mums trying to shift baby weight and other quick-fix dieters. What's really smart (or cynical depending on your point of view) is that this campaign also increased the frequency of consumption, as people were eating Special K for lunch and dinner. Clearly the diet was neither sensible, nutritious or worthwhile, but it did achieve one significant thing - it made the brand aspirational and synonymous with being slim, attractive and confident, broadening its appeal. Entering 2012, Special K is re-positioning again and moving away from the quick fix diet to enrolling dieters into a longer term nutritional plan, positioning the brand as a long term weight management solution. The cynics amongst you will note that this increases the frequency of consumption even further.

☐ Create the habit of scanning the papers or online news sites each morning looking for topical news stories you could leverage.

☐ Register with the sites looking for experts detailed in the resource box.

☐ What new distribution channels could you consider? Which companies are potential joint venture partners? Is a referral scheme right for your business?

☐ What could you do to extend the appeal of your brand? Could you create new occasions or situations to use your products and services? Or highlight an additional benefit, this could be existing feature you haven't yet talked about, or an extra service you could offer.

☐ Would your brand benefit from a re-positioning strategy? To what other audiences do you want to appeal and why?

RESOURCES

- **www.helpareporter.com** - More than 50,000 journalists use HARO to find experts for on-air interviews, article quotes and opinions. I also recommend joining their Facebook group.

- **https://profnet.prnewswire.com** - Profnet is a paid membership site linking reporters to expert sources

- **www.sourcebottle.com.au** - A free Australian service connecting journalists and experts from all over the world.

It's a numbers game

> "You can't run a business without understanding the numbers, you could be the most creative, inventive person in the whole world, but if you don't understand the numbers and cash flow, you're dead."
>
> **Theo Paphitis**

The most profitable thing you can ever do in your business is to understand the numbers. The devil really is in the detail when it comes to your business and marketing strategy. If you have the right business intelligence then you really do hold all of the answers in your hot little hands. So far, I've revealed the importance of making small, manageable changes that, when combined, create a much bigger difference to your all important bottom line. I now want to challenge the conventional business model that focuses on acquiring new customers at the lowest possible price. What if we turned this conventional thinking on its head and considered paying more to acquire our customers? Madness? We'll see.

Victoria is a greeting card designer, primarily selling her beautifully designed cards in bulk to retail customers. On average, a retail customer spends £200 at each sale and buys her new designs three times a year to sell in his or her store. Her relationship with each retailer lasts for five years on average, so the average lifecycle of each customer is five years, making the average lifetime revenue that Victoria receives £3,000:

£200 x 3 times a year x 5 years = £3,000

On average, it costs Victoria £75 in sales commission to acquire a new customer and other associated costs for each £200 order are £25, so on the first sale, Victoria's net profit is £100. There-after, as the sales commission is a one-off cost and the £25 is an ongoing cost, the net profit on each additional order is £175.

£200 - £25 = £175

Let's now calculate the lifetime net profit from her customer: (assuming costs stay the same each year)

	Order value		First sale costs		Second sale costs		Third sale costs		Net profit
Year 1:	£200 x 3	-	£100	-	£25	-	£25	=	£450
Year 2:	£200 x 3	-	£25	-	£25	-	£25	=	£525
Year 3:	£200 x 3	-	£25	-	£25	-	£25	=	£525
Year 4:	£200 x 3	-	£25	-	£25	-	£25	=	£525
Year 5:	£200 x 3	-	£25	-	£25	-	£25	=	£525
Total:	£3,000	-	£200	–	£125	-	£125	=	£2,550

On average, each retail customer is worth £2,550 in net profit. When Victoria understood this, she realised how short term her approach to commission was and agreed, initially, to double the commission that she paid to the sales guy for the first sale, so he received £150. Six months later, she tripled it and he received £225, this meant that Victoria made a loss on that first sale. Why? What do you think that this did to the motivation of the sales team? It went through the roof and she significantly increased her customer base. A win-win situation.

If you don't have a sales team and you sell directly to consumers, the same principles still apply, you just give the extra value to the consumer, instead of a sales guy. Create an irresistible offer for your consumers by bundling up other products or services to make that initial sale. Just remember that the first sale is nowhere near as valuable as the lifetime value of a customer and if you look at your customer acquisition strategy in this way, you will have a whole new perspective.

This is not a new strategy by any means. It's used by some of the most successful companies in the world. Think about credit cards and their 0% balance transfer strategy. Wine clubs offer the first crate of wines at rock bottom prices, book clubs offer a number of books at a fraction of the price. They all know that they make their money in the long term. They have all calculated the potential lifetime value of their customers and created the most desirable deal to entice them in. However, this strategy is not for everyone. A cash-strapped start-up would struggle to adopt this strategy, as cash flow is critical in the early stages and lowering customer acquisition costs is key.

ACTION

❑ Start by calculating the average spend per order, if you haven't done this already.

❑ Calculate *all* costs associated with that order, from marketing to sales commissions to production costs and work out the net profit per order. It's vital you get this right.

❑ Calculate the average frequency of purchase each year and look at how long, on average, a customer continues to buy from you.

❑ To calculate the lifetime value (or net profit) of a customer calculate the following:

  ❑ Average frequency of purchase each year x the average net profit x average no of years customers buy.

  ❑ If you have been in business for a few years and have a sales history, it is easier to calculate the above, but if you're just starting out, it's ok to make some conservative assumptions that you can review over time.

❑ Now think about how you could turn your customer acquisition strategy on its head. What would happen if you gave 100% commission to your sales team for the first sale? Or gave consumers unbelievable value on their first purchase with you? What could you offer that would lower the barriers to purchase to as close to zero as possible? Think long-term, not short-term and unleash the possibilities.

Why you need to approach daily deal sites with caution

> "We watch our competitors, learn from them, see what they are doing well for their customers and then copy as much as we can."
> **Jeff Bezos**

Daily deal sites have taken the UK by storm. Every day myriad of heavily discounted deals from wine tasting to massages and a whole lot more in between, are offered up to bargain hungry consumers. Groupon is the largest player and offers daily deals in more than 560 cities globally. In just sixteen months they went from launch to $1billion in valuation, YouTube is the only start up to achieve this more quickly (12 months). Groupon's quick success spawned a number of clones; Living Social, KGB Deals, Wahanda, LyncMeUp and many more.

SO HOW DOES IT WORK?

Daily deal sites bring buyers and sellers together and by promising a minimum number of customers for the vendor, they can offer deals that aren't otherwise available. The deal only goes live once enough people have bought it, which incentivises consumers to share the deal with everyone they know until "the deal is on." The consumer gets a great discount and the site takes a hefty commission.

Sounds great. No upfront marketing costs and a steady stream of customers with money drip feeding from the deal sites, as consumers take up the deal.

Well it can be, but it needs to be approached with caution. The explosion of collective buying sites offering cheap deals has encouraged a nation of promiscuous bargain hunters, loyal only to the deals. Not great for repeat business, clearly. Unless you have a strategy in place to drive repeat custom, then running a deal can be a one hit wonder and an expensive hit at that.

Here's an example; deals are usually discounted by 50%, so a restaurant that usually offers a three-course meal at £100 would offer this at £50 and then the deal site could take 50% of the deal price. In effect, the restaurant takes a 75% hit per meal. This is only sustainable if diners return, otherwise it is a very expensive customer acquisition strategy. What makes this even worse is that customers who ordinarily pay full price might buy the deal, crippling your margins further.

Don't get me wrong, I am not against running a daily deal, you just need to consider its role in your marketing mix very carefully. It's key to remember that competing on price doesn't get you love; high quality products and services that deliver unique and engaging experiences does. Deep discounts are bad for a brand's long-term health.

To make this channel work harder for you, consider the following tips:

Research the opportunity

Contact a similar company who has run a deal on the site and ask them a few key questions:

❑ How many of the deal customers were their existing customers?

❑ How big was the initial demand?

❑ Did they need to increase the number of staff to cope with the demand?

❑ Did people spend more than the value of the deal?

❑ Did new deal customers come back?

Plan your re-engagement strategy

The deal sites build their database, not yours, so ensure that you get the contact details for new customers. If they buy from you online then it's straightforward, but if your business is offline and they come in-store, you need to give them a reason to part with their details when they take up the offer. You should also encourage them to follow you on Twitter, or become a fan on Facebook, so that you can connect with them in the future.

Up-sell at point of purchase

Deal sites only take commission on the initial deal price, not on your up-sells. So don't be persuaded by the sales reps to increase the initial value of your deal by bundling more products or services; do so when you benefit 100% from the increased spend.

Don't promote the deal

Don't tweet or tell your Facebook fans about the deal, the objective is to get new customers, not give discounts to current.

Allow one deal per customer

If multiple deals are bought by the same person you will struggle to get repeat traffic at your usual prices. The deal should be the loss-leader designed to acquire new, repeat customers.

Be prepared

Make sure you have enough products and or staff to meet increased demand and consider increased hours of service. Make the most of the customer surge and offer additional product bundles.

Look after your regulars

If you're in the service industry, keep time slots available for your regular full-paying customers, call them in advance and give them the chance to book in before the busy period.

Deliver a great experience

Your goal is to drive repeat custom, so ensure deal customers have as great an experience as a full-paying customer.

Track and monitor the uptake

There will always be a few unscrupulous consumers who try to take the deal more than once by re-printing the voucher. Keep track of every voucher to avoid this eventuality.

Follow up

Once your new customers have taken up the deal, tell them about other services or products that you have and encourage them to come back as full-paying customers. Track how many actually do, as this is the true determinant of the success of a group deal campaign. Group discount deals can work to your advantage, but you have to be prepared and you have to analyse the results. Evaluate the return on investment of this type of promotion versus the others that you run and if it stacks up, go again.

ACTION

❑ Take a look at each of the daily deal sites, which one best suits your niche? What could you offer as a daily deal? What could you offer as an up-sell once they have bought the deal?

❑ Contact the sites you are interested in and contact companies in your niche that have run deals with them. Most of the deal sites have a "previous deals" section so you can identify relevant companies quite easily.

Strategies to increase frequency of purchase

> "Whenever you see a successful business, someone once made a courageous decision."
> **Peter Drucker**

It's really important to analyse purchasing patterns to identify the frequency that your customers buy your products and services. You need to understand not only the difference between your light, medium and heavy buyers, but also why your heavies use or consume so much more than your lights. These insights can help you to create strategies to move your lights to mediums and your mediums to heavies. That's the theory anyway, but in reality it is a bit more complicated than that. You might find that your segments respond differently to promotions, so make sure that you track the uptake of each strategy by segment to find the sweet spots.

FREQUENT COMMUNICATION

One of the biggest ways to increase a customer's frequency of purchase is actually one of the easiest. Frequent communication. Just because someone has bought from you once or twice, this is no guarantee that that they will buy from you again. You need to build a relationship and show that you care through regular communication that helps you to stay top of mind. Each month plan a communication calendar that details your key messages for the month by channel and stick to it. Intersperse one promotional message in every three and monitor the uptake for the month.

INCREASE VOLUME OF USAGE PER OCCASION

If you have a consumable product, how could you increase the amount that people use each time? Toothpaste manufacturers have been known to widen the opening, so that a larger amount is used each time someone brushes their teeth. To encourage buyers to eat more gum, Wrigley's encouraged people to share their gum through their "Great to chew, even better to share" campaign from years ago. In an earlier chapter I revealed how Lynx deodorants launched the "Spray more, get more" campaign that encouraged teenage boys to liberally apply the deodorant all over their body, not just under their arms, to increase their success with the opposite sex. This was very successful at increasing frequency of purchase. What could you do to encourage your buyers to consume more in one sitting?

EXTEND THE BUYING SEASON

Some hay-fever remedy manufacturers encourage sufferers to start taking their products before the hay-fever season kicks in, as a preventive measure. Naturally sufferers continue to take them through the season too, so this increases the frequency of their purchase each year. What could you do in your business, does the "prevention is better than cure" strategy apply? If you have a seasonal product, how could you extend that season?

LOYALTY SCHEMES

Loyalty schemes are a great way to drive up frequency, as customers are rewarded for every purchase that they make. As points accrue, they get closer to the rewards and they become more likely to choose your brand over the competition. A study into the psychology of loyalty schemes was conducted by Rajesh Bagchi and Xingbo Li in a paper for the February, 2011 issue of the *Journal of Consumer Research*. They identified that if consumers were given a high number of points for each purchase (10 points / $1 versus 1 point / $1) they were more excited by the scheme and more likely to tell other people about it, even when the amount they needed to spend to get a prize was exactly the same. That said, the quality and desirability of the rewards on offer determine the success of a loyalty scheme, but it is still worth bearing this in mind.

SPECIAL OFFERS

The most successful special offers tend to be those that create scarcity through limited availability. This can mean a limited time frame, such as "today only", or limited volume, "just one hundred available". It's vital you stick to your claims though, or you lose credibility. There are so many ways to create a special offer, they can be for everyone; seasonal sales, introductory offers, targeted birthday offers, 100th, 1,000th customer, etc. Track and evaluate uptake so that you identify and re-run only the most successful offers.

ACTION

❑ What promotional strategy could you run in the next four weeks to increase the frequency of purchase?

❑ Do you already have a loyalty programme in place, or do you need to create one? Either way, make sure that you offer multiple points per £1 spent.

Strategies to increase average order values

> "Success breeds complacency.
> Complacency breeds failure.
> Only the paranoid survive."
> **Andy Grove**

Managing cash flow can be a big problem when you first start out. Whilst there are myriad ways to address this, which are not the subject of this book, increasing average order value is a great way to ease this problem. Here are three strategies guaranteed to help your cash flow.

CROSS-SELLS

You can increase the average order value by cross-selling related items. Let's assume you sell shoes and on average a customer spends £65 on a pair of shoes. Typical cross-sells are cleaning products, protectors, shoehorns, inner soles. All of the products are directly related to what is being purchased, but they all focus on increasing customer spend at the point of purchase.

Amazon excels at this style of promotion. When buying anything, from a CD to a cuddly toy, Amazon lets you know that "people who bought this, also bought this" and suggests two or three additional products. It's incredibly successful and at times you're even grateful to Amazon for reminding you to buy that extra lead with your camera, as you didn't realise that it came without it. So you spend more and leave even more satisfied with their service. Genius.

What can you offer as a cross-sell at the point of purchase? Ensure it is relevant and adds genuine value. It is also advisable to offer discounts based on bundled purchases to further encourage take up. As always, ensure you track and monitor the impact of your cross-sells, week in, week out. If take up is low, then reconsider the products on offer.

UP-SELLS

An up-sell is when you encourage a customer to buy the more expensive version of a product or service. Up-sells are a key sales strategy for mobile phone providers; they have multiple packages of increasing value, based on more, or less air time, messages and Internet usage. If you are a masseuse, you could offer a three month massage package instead of a one-off. If you sell tickets to an event, you could include lunch or a drink at the bar for an increased ticket price. If you're an author you could sell your book with an accompanying audio tape. Taking this a stage further, you could bundle products and services together and create tiered pricing up-sells such as "Bronze", "Silver" and "Gold" packages of increasing value. This is a very effective way to drive up order values. If you only have one product or service, then explore joint venture partnerships to bundle up deals and, as usual, track and monitor uptake. Alternatively you could offer different priced packages based on different warranties or length of trial offers. Think about what makes sense for your business.

Discounts for multiple purchases made at once can be an effective way to increase the amount people spend, but you need to find the sweet spot for your industry. Retailers frequently promote volume discounts, such as "buy one get one free" and "three for two" deals. Retailers also offer percentage discounts for multiple purchases, these are often the same deals, just expressed differently and generating a different success rate. Just take a look at the shelves and you will see the variations. You need to analyse the numbers and then start experimenting and tracking all the results. Start by looking at what your competitors are doing, promotions that run frequently, are usually the most effective.

INCREASE YOUR PRICES

I frequently notice a real nervousness when I suggest increasing a client's prices. It usually stems from a fear of losing customers to the competition. Justified you might think and you possibly harbour that same fear. However, chances are, like my clients, you offer a great product or service, as there is little place for mediocrity in today's harsh business environment, and this presents a great opportunity. It's possible that in doubling your prices you will halve your customer base, but this is actually a great result, particularly if you're in a service industry as you now have a lot more free time and the same amount of income. Now I am not advocating this strategy, as it is clearly not for everyone. However, what would happen if you increased your prices by just 1% or 2% overnight? I can answer this for you. Usually nothing at all, well except a greater cash flow into your business that is. So do the sums, what impact would an increase of 1% - 5% do for you? Push yourself, what about 10% or 20%?

Alternatively you can "premiumise" your product or services and add extra value to justify extra price. Gillette is phenomenal at this; every razor launched has a new functionality over and above the last. The cost for each is increased as a result.

ACTION

❑ Make a list of potential products or services that you could cross-sell, both your own and through joint venture partners.

❑ Now list the main brands that manufacture or offer these products and services.

❑ Contact each company and ask if they would be interested in a new distribution channel. Your distribution channel.

❑ Consider how you could combine your products or services into bronze, silver and gold packages?

❑ Calculate the impact a price increase of 1% - 5% would have on your cash flow?

❑ Now raise your prices.

Customer retention strategies

> "There is only one boss; the customer.
> And he can fire everybody in the company
> from the chairman on down, simply by
> spending his money somewhere else."
> **Sam Walton, Founder of Walmart**

Identifying ways to retain your most profitable customers is often overlooked in the excitement of acquiring them. In the last chapter you calculated the lifetime value of a customer, so you have realised the importance of retaining as many of your customers as possible. Companies that retain 100% of a growing customer base are incredibly rare. Invariably you will lose some customers over the course of the year, but a few simple steps can help you to minimise this rate of attrition.

Most business owners know exactly how many new customers they win month in, month out, but fail to track how many they lose. To do this you need to agree on the definition of a lapsed customer and this depends on the nature of your business. As I outlined in the earlier chapter, "The six reasons your customers leave you", you start by identifying the average buying cycles for each of your niches and the time period that indicates that they are now a lapsed customer, which could be three, six or twelve months depending on your business. You then need to track how many customers you lose over this time period and calculate the amount of revenue you lose by just letting them slip away. Spend a moment to calculate how many customers you lose on average each year. Based on the lifetime value of a customer how much revenue are you missing out on? How much would you retain if you reduce the number of customers who leave you by 10% a year. Yes, it's the "10% strategy" again.

Go on, get the calculator out.

Done? Good. Now you know why you need a retention strategy!

It's important to identify the volume of lapsed customers for each niche and compare the results. What can you learn about the type of customers who defect? Are there trends in the data? If so, these should feed into your acquisition strategy, as there is little point spending money acquiring particular customers that defect after a couple of months. It's also critical to find out why they defect, as mentioned earlier, dissenting customers can inform you on how you can improve your product or service.

LOYALTY VERSUS PROFITABILITY

It is often ill advised to try to target too many niches. Remember Pareto's 80:20 law? The lion's share (80%) of anything is created by a few (20%). When applied to your business, it's highly likely that 20% of your customers are delivering 80% of your profits. Don't waste those profits chasing unprofitable niches. As your cost to acquire, serve and retain a consumer in each of your niches is more or less the same, you need to prioritise and focus on retaining customers that are actually making you money, not costing you.

CUSTOMER RETENTION STRATEGIES

Connect and communicate regularly

This is the single, most important, strategy. In the chapter: "The six reasons your customers leave you" I revealed that the biggest reason is perceived indifference. It's so important to show that you genuinely appreciate their business. A regular newsletter, blog or connecting via social media are great ways to do this and to keep your brand top of mind.

Deliver extraordinary customer service

Deliver better than expected levels of customer service to each and every customer. Go beyond the call of duty and not only will you retain your existing customers, but they will tell others just how great it is to do business with you. Respond immediately to any issues, always deliver what you promise before and after a sale and critically hire brilliant people to deliver a service you can be proud of.

Treat complaints as a gift

96% of customers who leave you, will never tell you why. When someone does complain, listen and act on it. You now have the perfect opportunity to surprise and delight them and even potentially to turn them into an advocate. Make sure it is easy for customers to complain and suggest improvements.

Run regular surveys

Ask for feedback on a regular basis, it can be a great way to prevent a niggle becoming a problem.

Create a loyalty scheme

This is an effective form of retention if, as discussed in an earlier chapter, you offer desirable rewards, your customers will willingly sign-up.

ACTION

❏ If you haven't done this already, identify how many customers you lose each year and calculate what retaining just 10% of them would do to your bottom line.

❏ Decide on a strategy that you could put in place tomorrow to lower your rate of defection.

How to measure ROI
(Return on Investment)

> "Half of my advertising budget is wasted, I
> just don't know which half."
> **David Ogilvy**

As I think you might have realised by now, I am obsessed with numbers and analytics. If you want to grow your business and get results, you will need to share my obsession, or hire someone who does. When you first launch a company, you don't really know what will work in your sector when it comes to marketing. You might know what your competitors are doing, but you don't always know whether their strategies are truly generating results. Even when you do have that insight, what works for another, more established brand, might not work for your brand spanking new one. When there are a number of variables at play, there is only one way to move forward with certainty. Testing. It's the only way to identify the most effective strategy that produces the greatest results for the lowest returns on time, money and effort.

NEVER, EVER ASSUME

Subjectivity is dangerous. It will cost you money. A lot of money. The only way to identify the best approach is to evaluate all of the alternatives. It's difficult to argue with facts, they stare back up at you in all their black and white glory. You either made a sale or you didn't. Facts. I love them. You will too, as soon as you see what they can do for your business.

A TESTER'S WORK IS NEVER DONE

You need to test *every* part of your marketing; prices, bundles, headlines, copy, packaging – every single element. Where you run your ads or distribute your products or services, also needs to be analysed, as well as all the elements of your website; is your "buy" button more effective on the right or the left, in red or in green? If you sell offline, test your sales patter, what happens when you open and close differently? You need to review the impact of every change on your conversion of suspects, to prospects to customers. What does each tweak do to the average cost of sale, the frequency of purchase and the profit per sale? If you have no idea where you stand on any of the above right now, then today's the day to start. You need to establish your benchmarks, so that you can monitor the improvements that are guaranteed from the rigorous testing you are about to put in place.

Unfortunately, you don't have an infinite supply of time or money, so finding how to do more with less is key. If you have a fixed monthly marketing budget, wouldn't you rather maximise the return on every effort? If you have a sales team that can physically only make a certain number of calls a day, wouldn't you rather increase their conversions? Of course you would. So why not test a new approach every day, or every week? Add or change a guarantee, create a new product or service bundle, add a new up-sell, play with the price and then monitor the results. If a strategy delivers better results, it becomes the new benchmark and the testing continues. Some strategies will yield lower results, but until you test, you can't know this. Don't be disheartened, it's not failure, it's feedback and the sky is the limit when it comes to this process. It's important to avoid complacency and think that the results you are getting are "good enough". What if they are actually mediocre or poor, versus where you could push through to?

When testing your advertising, you need to make sure that you can identify which channels and which ads are driving greater sales. If the call to action is to contact you by phone, use a different phone number on each ad to track call volumes. This way you can identify which publication, or advertising channel is more effective. If you sell your products and services online, create a different discount code for each channel, so you can track whether Facebook promotions deliver more sales that Twitter and so on. Test and test and test again.

MINIMISE YOUR RISKS

If you keep the test market small you can minimise your risk. You might have a subscriber base of 40,000, but run an A/B split test amongst just 2,000 and monitor the results before you roll it out. If you want to run an ad in a national paper, test it regionally first, the same goes for radio. You will always end up with more sales and more enquiries from testing ads against each other, as there will always be one winner.

THINK LONG TERM

Different ads or strategies can lead to different long-term buying behaviour. The only way to identify this is to track and analyse results. One of my clients discarded ads that were outperformed, but when we analysed the repeat buying behaviour of customers that came through the lower performing ad, we noticed that their lifetime value was greater than for customers that came from the better performing ad. An important insight. You need to develop a very rigorous approach to testing your communications and I recommend tracking and monitoring the following for each ad and channel monthly, quarterly and yearly if required:

- ❏ Volume of sales
- ❏ Value of sales
- ❏ Average order value
- ❏ Profit per customer
- ❏ Frequency of purchase

Make sure that you clearly identify the changes that lead to each set of results.

You need to be equally rigorous when it comes to your sales presentations, so in addition to the above track the following:

- ❑ Number of meetings
- ❑ % of closures
- ❑ Ensure that you use the same sales team to test new sales presentations each time, so as not to skew the results, as some sales people are naturally more effective than others.
- ❑ If all of this just sounds exhausting, then consider outsourcing your marketing, hire someone who will take a rigorous approach to your marketing and they will pay for themselves over and over again.

ACTION

- ❑ Review your business and list all the ways that you could A/B test performance.
- ❑ Now prioritise each activity and start to roll them out one by one. Remember to only change one variable at a time and to keep a strict track record of what changes and the results it delivers.
- ❑ If you're not doing it already, start analysing your sales success; volume of calls, volume of meetings, volume of sales, value of sales, average order value, what up-sells and cross sells have the greatest take up, which the least? If you're not measuring it, you're not managing it.

CONCLUSION

Revisiting the 10% Strategy

> "The brave may not live forever, but the
> cautious don't live at all."
> **Richard Branson**

At the start of this book, I introduced you to the "10% strategy" and showed you how small changes can make a big difference to your bottom line. The strategies that I have outlined over the course of this book have focused on helping you to improve every single one of these metrics. To make it easy for you to get started, below details each key metric and the strategies that you can follow to improve it.

HOW TO IMPROVE THE QUALITY OF YOUR LEADS

The quality of your leads determines the success of your whole marketing funnel. Following are the strategies I outlined that can help you to attract the right leads:

Cement your positioning through free content

❑ What you giveaway needs to "un-target" time wasters and non-buyers.

Customer referral programmes

❑ If your customers love what you do, chances are their connections will too, so incentivise them to shout from the rooftops about your brand.

Influence the influencer programmes

❑ Identify and connect with the key influencers in your industry, think long term and build relationships, don't be salesy.

Make your content easy to share

❑ Add social sharing buttons to your website and blog and encourage people to share your content at the end of your articles and posts.

Get your brand talked about by the Media

❑ Scan the news for topical articles you could comment on and call up the news desks.

❑ Sign-up as an expert on sites like HARO and receive alerts from journalists looking for experts.

HOW TO IMPROVE YOUR CONVERSIONS

Turning leads into customers is a critical role for your marketing and you should strive to continually improve your conversions.

Track and optimise everything

❑ Sometimes the smallest details make the biggest difference, so don't be complacent. Treat your sales and marketing as though they are always in beta. As a minimum, test one thing every single month.

Create relationships, don't focus on transactions

❑ People want to buy from brands they know, like and trust, so ensure your approach to marketing is social and creates real connections.

Increase the number of "touches" you have with prospects

❑ Google's research showed that consumers use more than ten sources of information to make a decision. How many do you have? Vary your content and use multiple channels.

Create keyword targeted communications

❑ The more specific and niche your communication is, the higher your conversions. Outline the problems and issues that your products and services address and create relevant and engaging content around them.

Share social proof

❑ Hearing about someone else's positive experience with your brand is a great way to improve conversions. Get as many testimonials as you can, ideally video, but for written testimonials include photos and their full name for greater credibility.

HOW TO INCREASE YOUR AVERAGE ORDER VALUE

A cash-flow crisis is one of the biggest reasons start ups fail. Focusing on strategies that increase the average spend can help you to avoid running dry.

Up-sells

❑ How could you create tiered offerings; product or service bundles with increasing price points? Each tier needs to offer such great value, it is a no-brainer to spend that bit more.

Cross-sells

❑ What relevant and related products or services could you offer your consumers at the point of purchase? With whom could you create a joint venture partnership to make it happen?

Increase your prices

❑ This is often thought of as the easiest way to avert a cash-flow crisis, but it comes with a risk. Increasing your prices can mean losing customers. Analyse the numbers, what could your business tolerate? If you increased your prices by 5% and lost 1% of your customers what would that do to your bottom line? Obviously you don't want to lose any, but if your company needs a cash injection this might be an important strategy.

HOW TO INCREASE THE FREQUENCY OF PURCHASE

Create frequent communications

❑ Keep your brand top of mind through timely communications, intersperse relevant, engaging and useful content with promotions .

Create a loyalty programme

❑ Loyalty programmes are proven to increase the number of times someone buys from you each year. They used to be incredibly expensive to set up, but now companies like Referral Candy have made them accessible to all businesses.

Increase the volume consumed on each occasion

❑ If you have a consumable product could you encourage buyers to use more of it in one sitting?

Extend the buying period

❑ If your product or service is seasonal how could you extend its use beyond the season?

HOW TO IMPROVE YOUR MARGINS

Improve customer retention

❑ When customers switch to a competitor, it hits you where it hurts. To minimise losses, you have to build strong relationships with your customers, if they feel valued, they are much more likely to stay.

❑ Look at your approach to customer service, how could you improve it? How could you surprise and delight your customers in unexpected ways?

Analyse the effectiveness of your marketing

❑ Your marketing needs to make you money, not drain it. Make sure that you can measure the effectiveness of every piece of marketing, I say this repeatedly, but it is important, if you are not measuring it, you are not managing it. You need to be able to identify which channels deliver the greatest returns, so that you can increase spend in them and decrease the poor performers.

Analyse the effectiveness of your sales approach

❑ Start tracking important metrics so that you can identify weak spots in your sales approach. How many calls lead to a meeting, how many meetings lead to a sale? Test different opening and closing techniques, different up-sells, product or service bundles and so on.

Analyse the cost of doing business

❑ Whilst this wasn't a focus of the book, it's still a key consideration. It's important to review all of the costs in your business, from your office rent to what it costs you to produce your products and services and see how you can lower them to improve your profit margin. I recommend doing this once a year, as a minimum.

ACTION

❑ Set yourself a goal of improving your metrics by 10%, start with your leads, create a strategy focused on delivering 10% more leads into the top of your funnel, then move on to improving your conversions by 10% and then your average order value. This is achievable in twelve months and, for the focused, in six! Note today's date and put a reminder in your calendar in six and twelve months time to send me an email at Jacqueline@jacquelinebiggs.com to let me know how you got on.

Final thoughts

> "You can't run a business on hope.
> You can run a business on plans,
> lots of passion, pain and anguish,
> and if you don't, it's a hobby."
> **Theo Paphitis**

EFFECTIVE MARKETING = PROCESS + MAGIC

To be an effective marketer you need a process. It takes a lot of hard work, dedication and due diligence. You need to obsess about the detail and know your numbers inside out. That said, sometimes the biggest breakthroughs have nothing to do with strategic planning, they are down to luck and a bit of magic that meant a company was in the right place at the right time to capitalise on a trend or an opportunity. You can't plan for these big breaks, they are too infrequent and unpredictable, but what you can do is improve your current marketing by testing, testing and testing some more.

I am often asked if there is a secret to my marketing process and, as you have evidenced over the course of this book, the "secret" is hard work and analysis. It's not a secret, but most people just don't do it. Which is why, if you follow the strategies that I have outlined, you will surpass your competitors.

That said, there are a few principles that I always share with my clients:

Keep your promises

I hope this sounds really obvious. It should do. If you say your customer service is excellent, then make sure it is. If you say you deliver in twenty-four hours, make sure you do.

Nobody gets it right first time

Tomorrow will always improve on today. Effective marketers are always in beta.

Go with your gut

You know your business better than anyone. Go with your gut, test it, evaluate it and do more of it when it's brilliant.

Get focused

When you start out, pick one niche and be laser targeted. Don't ever try and be all things to all people.

Be obsessive

The devil is in the detail and when you stop obsessing you start declining.

Never compromise on marketing

Diluting your ideas is dangerous. Half of idea A plus half of idea B = a disaster. Be confident and test the extremes. If you don't push your boundaries you will never know what you could achieve.

Test test test

Test, evaluate and optimise - this will bring you success in the long term.

Never stop learning

Don't ever become complacent. The world is changing so fast and if you choose to stand still, you will be forgotten. I read at least one business book a week that challenges me and changes my perspective.

THANK YOU FOR READING

So that's it, it's now over to you. I hope that I have inspired you to make the most of what you have, to ramp up your marketing and propel your business forward. To access additional content and more marketing tips go to:

www.JacquelineBiggs.com

I would love to hear your success stories, your breakthroughs and how you apply these strategies to your business. Don't be a stranger, email me at: jacqueline@jacquelinebiggs.com

Just remember, there is no failure, except in no longer trying. Now go out there and win!

PS If you enjoyed the book, please leave me a review on Amazon, as reviews are really important to authors.

Bibliography

I read a lot of business books and many have influenced me over the years so I thought I would share my favourites so you can continue your education. In no particular order:

The Four Hour Work Week, Tim Ferriss

Good To Great: Why Some Companies Make The Leap And Others Don't, Jim Collins

Built To Last: Successful Habits Of Visionary Companies, Jim Collins

Trust Me, I'm Lying: Confessions Of A Media Manipulator, Ryan Holliday

All Marketers Are Liars, Seth Godin

Tribes: We Need You To Lead Us, Seth Godin

Permission Marketing, Seth Godin

The Purple Cow: Transform Your Business By Being Remarkable, Seth Godin

The Tipping Point: How Little Things Can Make A Big Difference, Malcolm Gladwell

Blink: The Power Of Thinking Without Thinking, Malcolm Gladwell

Ogilvy On Advertising, David Ogilvy

Positioning: The Battle For Your Mind, Al Ries and Jack Trout

The Lean Startup, Eric Ries

Creative Mischief, Dave Trott

The Brand Gap, Marty Neumeier

Brand Failures, Matt Haig

Scientific Advertising, Claude.C.Hopkins

Re-Work: Change The Way You Work Forever, Jason Fried and David Heinemeier Hansson

Understanding Brands By 10 People Who Do, Don Cowley

Trust Agents: Using The Web To Build Influence, Improve Reputation & Earn Trust, Chris Brogan and Julien Smith

The E-Myth Revisited, Michael Gerber

Marketing in the Era of Accountability, Les Binet and Peter Fields

Acknowledgements

Writing a book is a massive undertaking and at risk of this feeling like a gushy Oscar's speech, there are a lot of people to thank. Without the support of my amazing friends and family, I don't think I could have finished Marketing to Win.

This book is dedicated to my amazing parents, Anne and Ken Biggs, as their continual encouragement and support spurred me on to the end. Thanks also goes to my Aunty Mary and John for continually believing in me.

I locked myself away for many, many weekends and nights and whenever I needed to re-enter the real world, there was always someone on hand to pour me a glass of wine. Corinne, Rob, Theresa, Jen, Graham, Anna – thank you, thank you, thank you.

A big thanks goes to my brilliant big sister, Victoria, your feedback on the early draft was invaluable, as were the many, many discussions that followed.

The book cover was designed by the amazing team at www.ThisIsOrb.com, so a huge thank you to my amazing business partner, Rob Bloxham and his team Sanj Sahota, Jim Rogers, Ant Jones & Lauren Gamlin.

Thanks also to Tim Ferriss and all my Kimono friends, the inspiration and amazing advice I'm so privileged to have access to has been invaluable. Valerie Khoo deserves a special mention for spending so much time reading, evaluating and advising me on the early draft.

Thanks also goes to the other readers of my early drafts, Paulina Sygulska, Mary Murray, Devron Cariba, Steve Greenfield and Nigel Quantick.

Lucy, my publisher at Rethink Press, thank you for getting me organised and answering my many, many questions.

And finally, my KPI friends, thank you for sharing this journey with me and Daniel and Mindy, thank you for making me get this book out of my head and into the hands of so many business owners.

Lightning Source UK Ltd.
Milton Keynes UK
UKOW051843210313

208014UK00015B/541/P